British
Townscapes

To my parents

8-8-72

British Townscapes

EWART JOHNS

With drawings by the author

London : Edward Arnold (Publishers) Ltd.

© Ewart Johns 1965
First published 1965

SET IN MONOPHOTO BASKERVILLE AND PRINTED BY OFFSET IN GREAT BRITAIN
BY WILLIAM CLOWES AND SONS, LIMITED, LONDON AND BECCLES

Preface

In an age equipped with both the desire and the means to effect an unprecedented amount of physical planning in towns, contributions to the study of urban shape naturally abound. Although there is a considerable amount of literature relating to the subject of town form, this seems to fall very broadly into two categories, one with an architectural leaning, and one of geographical flavour. Many geographers look at towns chiefly in plan form, and equate the shape of towns with the street patterns, the plans of houses and house plots, and the general outline of settlement as it appears on maps. Writers who look at towns from an architect's standpoint usually see them in terms of the qualities of the shapes and spaces which are seen from the ground level. The characteristic geographical approach omits the study of that part of town form which is there because men have always liked to consider shape as a thing that pleases the senses as well as providing for other needs: the architect-writer, in seeking a currently fashionable ideal, may miss some of the potent shapes that have been produced where a decent place in which to live has been hard-won from a tough environment of industrial bleakness or of suburban monotony. If we are to build new towns, re-make old ones and rear the sort of planners who can do these things without destroying the indefinable qualities that make a good urban environment we must provide in our education for a fuller understanding of our urban inheritance, including what we have been bequeathed of town shapes. This book looks at this inheritance from the point of view of a geographer in whom shape produces a strong aesthetic reaction: it is chiefly about the way in which urban shape is always subject, to a greater or lesser degree, to the demands of current fashion in design, and at the same time it seeks in some measure to remind the designer of towns of the background of physical and economic conditions against which builders have always had to work.

My most grateful thanks are due to Miss K. M. Dexter of the Department of English in the University of Exeter, whose counsel and encouragement have been companions to every stage of the writing of this book. To her I owe the experience that every teacher should know from time to time—that of becoming once again a student. Through her I have learned a new respect for the craft of writing, to which I have served a humble apprenticeship. The respect with which, in her turn, she has treated the aims of my work has been a generous reward for a pupil who has tried to justify the faith of his teacher.

I am much indebted to Professor W. G. Hoskins for reading the final manuscript and making a number of very helpful suggestions. I should like to thank the University of Exeter for financial assistance towards the expenses involved in collecting material for this book, and Professor Arthur Davies and other friends in the Department of Geography in that University for their ready help in a variety of ways during the time of its preparation. I gratefully acknowledge the kind help which I have received from Miss Marion Bethel in preparing type-scripts, and thank Mr. Rodney Fry for drawing certain maps, Miss Pamela Foulkes for her excellent typing services, and Dr. A. H. Shorter and Dr. K. J. Gregory for their work in the preparation of the index. I should like to thank Mr. Bernard Chapman for taking more than a professional interest in the photographic printing which he has done for this book, and Miss Margaret Bacon for rendering enthusiastic help on numerous occasions. Finally, and most of all, I would like to thank my wife for the many ways in which she has proved her awareness of a writer's private struggles.

Acknowledgements

Acknowledgement is due to the following for permission to use the indicated copyright illustrations:

The Controller of H.M. Stationery Office (Crown Copyright reserved) for Figs. 24, 36, 42, 47, 53, 55, 76, 96, 117, 120, 122, 126, 141, 149, 150; Aerofilms for Figs. 22, 24, 38, 43, 48, 52, 61, 62, 65, 66, 70, 71, 82, 97, 123, 124, 134, 147, 148, 152, 161, 162; Paul Popper for Fig. 6; The American Geographical Society for Fig. 3 (from R.U. Light: *Focus on Africa*); The Johannesburg Publicity Association for Fig. 4; The American School of Classical Studies at Athens and Professor H. A. Thompson for Fig. 5; East London Papers, Vol. 1, No. 1, for Fig. 8; Presses Universitaires de France for Figs. 10 and 19 (from Pierre George: *Précis de Géographie Urbaine*); The State of California Division of Highways for Fig. 11; The Herbert Art Gallery and Museum for Fig. 33; The Guildhall, Exeter for Fig. 35; The Trustees of the British Museum for Figs. 46, 51a and 51b; The Plymouth Corporation for Fig. 54 (from Watson & Abercrombie: *A Plan for Plymouth*, Underhill, Plymouth); The Royal Institute of British Architects for Figs. 58 and 113; The Royal Air Force (Crown Copyright reserved) for Fig. 114; *The Guardian* for Fig. 125; Mr. W. Schomberg Scott, A.R.I.B.A., for Fig. 69; The British Travel & Holidays Association for Fig. 84; Sir John Summerson and The Cresset Press for Figs. 64 and 86 (from *Georgian London*); The Corporation of Harrogate for Fig. 130 (from J. A. Patmore: *An Atlas of Harrogate*); The Cumbernauld Development Corporation for Fig. 169; The University of Wisconsin Press for Fig. 13 (from G. Trewartha: *Japan*); Mr. J. Allan Cash, F.I.B.P., F.R.P.S., for Fig. 18; The High Commissioner for New Zealand for Fig. 14; Routledge & Kegan Paul for Fig. 7 (from R. E. Dickinson: *The West European City*); The Architectural Press for Figs. 9 (from G. Cullen: *Townscape*), 165 (from F. Gibbard: *Town Design*) and 178 (from T. Sharp: *Exeter Phoenix*); K.L.M. for Fig. 20; Methuen for Fig. 25 (from T. D. Atkinson: *English Architecture*) and Fig. 73 (from E. W. Gilbert: *Brighton*); The Institute of British Geographers for Fig. 37 (Publication No. 27); Faber & Faber for Fig. 60 (from W. Ison: *The Georgian Buildings of Bath*); Oliver & Boyd for Fig. 68 (from I. Lindsay: *Georgian Edinburgh*); The Courier Press for Fig. 81 (from H. G. Clarke: *Royal Leamington Spa*); Hodder & Stoughton for Fig. 90 (from R. Millward: *Lancashire*); Tillotsons (Bolton) for Fig. 92 (from C. H. Saxelby: *Bolton Survey*); J. M. Dent & Sons for Fig. 140 (from C. B. Purdom: *The Letchworth Achievement*); The architects Barry Parker and Raymond Unwin for Fig. 143; George Wittenborn Inc. for Fig. 163; *Town & Country Planning*, July 1964, for Fig. 180 (from Ewart Johns: *Old and New Townscapes in Exeter*).

All illustrations not acknowledged above are by the author.

Contents

List of Illustrations

1. *Introduction*

A TOWN "belongs"—in a sense—to all who live in it and to all who use it. A book on towns, unless it is a highly technical one, should therefore be of interest to a wide range of readers whether their work involves them directly in town-affairs or not, and it is intended that this one shall appeal to such a varied audience. The central theme of *British Townscapes* is the way in which the tendency to shape the urban environment according to the fashion of the times survives, in characteristic form, in our towns to-day. Such a theme is of more than professional concern, for not only architects and builders, but also house-decorators, shopkeepers, lighting engineers, jobbing-plumbers and everyone who paints his garden gate, are responsible for the final appearance of the "landscape" of the towns in which we live. And, as very few people make no contribution at all to the shapes and colours of the public scenery around them, there is good reason for most of us to take a personal interest in the extent to which our surroundings are dictated by some kind of common "design-sense", some prevailing mode of making shapes and of using colours.

Throughout history, and, archaeology can assure us, throughout much of pre-history also, man has designed his villages, his towns and his cities not only for protection, comfort and economy, but also, in some measure, for the satisfaction of his sense of the propriety of the shapes in which he and his family should live. Although it has often been said, in the present century, that the proper criterion by which any design should be assessed is its "fitness for purpose", there is, abundantly shown on all sides in our streets and homes, a stubborn resistance in people to this clinical judgment. Of course an industrial landscape, in which almost every shape in view seems to be the product of the adaptation of materials to a specialised need—like the chimneys, turbine houses, pylons and cables of an electricity-generating station —can be a most dramatic and moving sight, and it may be said, with every justification, that such a scene has greater beauty than the dull forms of, for example, an uninspired-looking suburban shopping-street. But it is not our concern to pose the eternal question "What is beauty?": it is to show that attempts are always being made to enlarge upon the limits set on what is merely useful. Industrial buildings

I

Fig. 1. The factory of Storey Bros, Lancaster

have been considerably influenced by period styles (fig. 1) and the residential and commercial parts of our towns are even more affected in some way by our urge to design for design's sake (fig. 2). However much this assertion may seem to favour "arty" notions, there is evidence around us everywhere that only a minority has ever believed that town-building could, or should, be a process of trying to arrive at the ultimately perfect functional shape—unless, that is, we are to include in "function" the need to satisfy our urge to balance, to mould, to colour and to decorate—an instinctive desire, the cause of which no one has ever yet been able to explain.

2

Fig. 2. The Victorian town centre of Tavistock

Even if the shapes in contemporary towns sometimes fool us into thinking that they are purely functional—just because they are straight-lined and clean—there can be no doubt that the verdict of history is that towns are, amongst other things, the sculptural product of all the varied aspirations of a society. If we reduce buildings to their bare essentials we find that the basic shape of most structures, even to-day, is that of the box. This shape has, of course, been in use since the first towns came into being: it was used in the ancient cities of the Indus Plain and of Mesopotamia and Egypt; it was formed from dried mud, and was at times distorted to fit the irregularities of a site, or elaborated to enable it to serve the needs of a great

palace or of a defensive wall. The same shape exists to-day as the basic unit of much
twentieth-century building; tower-blocks and skyscrapers, commercial, factory and
residential buildings all have strongly-marked rectilinear plans and elevations, with
very little surface decoration (figs. 3 and 4). But in between these two phases of
urban design, where first impressions suggest that building is near to functional
perfection, are to be found the main results of the town-building process in which
every possible use of building materials as modelling substances seems to have been
exploited—from the refined geometry of the Greek city to the fantasies of the movement called Art Nouveau (figs. 5 and 6). Our notions of what is "proper" in the
shape of a building (beyond, that is to say, the form which satisfies our need for
shelter, warmth, and the accommodation of the principal private and social acts)
are governed by the powerful force of taste, a nebulous compound representing the
cumulative influences of moral and aesthetic judgments on what makes a good
appearance.[1] Taste will guide not only the architects of cathedrals and great public
buildings, but also, though less directly or powerfully, the builders of the more
humble parts of the town. Even a home-made garden shed, or a squatter's hut, may
embrace some of the prevailing ideas of good taste.

It will be the purpose of later chapters to justify these claims of the significance
of the element of architectural design in the whole townscape in Britain. Meanwhile,
perhaps enough has been said to show that the theme of the book is one of general
rather than of specialised interest. It is also to be hoped that this theme will help to
break some new ground in a field of very great topical concern, parts of which are,
by virtue of this concern, in some danger of becoming overcropped. The initial
inspiration to write this book came from a desire to help fill the gap between the
studies of towns made by architectural historians, and those made by geographers.
Books on architecture are often governed by the need to make value-judgments as
to the merits of various buildings, and they are concerned, as are the studies of art
historians, with assessing and reassessing the principal contributions of each phase
of design to the whole history of art. The result is that such works have little time to
spare for minor buildings, and none at all for bad ones.[2] Now where towns are
concerned, the best buildings, in the architectural sense, are always very limited in
number, while the more modest ones, and unfortunately the bad ones, too, cover
very extensive areas indeed. Since a student of towns must not ignore parts of the
townscape just because they are dull or even positively unattractive, he is free to explore in less obvious places than civic centres or the residential areas of the eighteenth century. (If in doing so he finds some townscapes to have unsuspected quality,
these discoveries alone may justify the exploration.) In any case, it would seem that
to the usual architectural studies of towns we could profitably add something which
seeks out the unobtrusive, as well as the more obvious, effects of changing architectural taste.

The geographer's studies of towns are much more comprehensive, in the
physical sense, than are those of the architectural historian. Chiefly because the
geographer so often looks at his subject "from above", that is to say in map form,
it is comparatively easy for him to get a complete picture of some aspects of a town.

Fig. 3. Minshat el Bakkari, near Giza, Egypt

Fig. 4. Part of Johannesburg today

Fig. 5. Model of the Agora
of Ancient Athens

Fig. 6. Sagrada Familia,
Barcelona, by Gaudi

When he applies his predilection for plans and spatial patterns to an architectural subject he may produce such aids to the study of townscapes as—for example—the map of building periods in Basel (fig. 7). As a rule the urban geographer translates most of the phenomena of the town into maps, for the purpose of analysis, and it would probably be fair to say that the more "mappable" an element of a town may be, the more it is likely to appeal to him. Thus we have, as characteristic subjects of study in urban geography, the relief and other physical conditions of the site of the town; the patterns of land-use—or as they are often called, the functional zones—of the town; the various characteristics of the plans of buildings and building-plots, and many other such themes. In recent years there has been increasing interest in what is known as *urban morphology* which is concerned, rather more closely than were previous studies in the geography of towns, with the actual shapes that the town makes on the ground. Thus we have the work of Professor A. E. Smailes, in which he takes the analysis of buildings beyond the usual limits, and attempts to express, cartographically, the visual effects of whole areas of buildings on the landscape. In fig. 8 we are shown a part of London's "Urban Texture" by means of a map of areas of "Block Clumping", "Ribbing" and "Studding", terms which represent, respectively, the high buildings which coalesce at the heart of built-up areas, the successive periods of terrace-housing, and the various regions which are character-ised by scattered units.

Fig. 7. Architectural periods of Basel (from Schaefer) (1) Medieval (Gothic) up to 1500. (2) Renaissance, 16th century. (3) Baroque and Classical, 1600–1800. (4) Neo-Romanesque, Neo-Gothic, and Neo-Classical, 1800–50. (5) Modern, since 1850. (6) Technical and Industrial. (7) Churches. (8) Open Spaces and Parks

Fig. 8. Urban texture in East London (after Smailes)

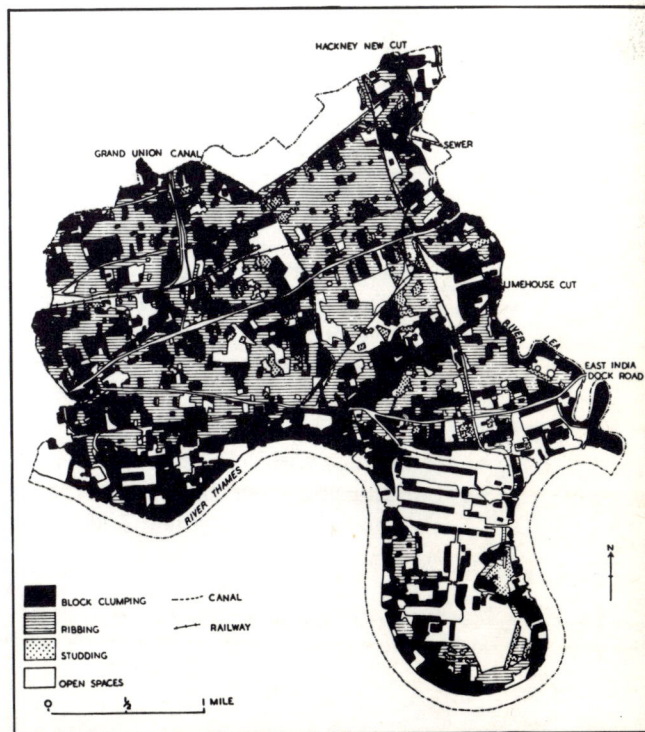

This work by Professor Smailes must surely lead to the mapping of architectural styles as one of the next steps in studies of his kind of townscape, and since geographers are interested in the whole town and not merely in the best-designed part of it, it may be for them to explore the influence of the principal phases of taste in shaping minor buildings as well as major ones. Certainly a geographer with a particular interest in architecture will find such a development of his subject a natural one. This book is not intended as a piece of original geographical research, and no attempt will be made to postulate a standard method for the mapping of architectural regions (or regions of "period-design", as they might be more correctly called): but if it draws attention to the importance of the element of design in the shape of towns, and if it should lead to a more analytical approach to this undoubtedly important part of the morphology of towns, it will have served one useful purpose.

The student of architecture, then, may well have something to learn from the wide-ranging and balanced view of the geographer, while the latter may take note of the fact that towns are shaped as they are, not only because of their site and their functions, but very much, too, because architects, planners and builders have been at work in greater or lesser degree throughout history.

At this point the clarification of some of the terms to be used throughout the book seems desirable. Planners and architects, geographers, sociologists and the general public, all use terms like "urban design",[3] "urban-nucleus", "town plan", "suburban", and a host of words which, although they may have slightly different meanings in different contexts, are widely understood and should cause no difficulty here. The problem of the word "architecture" has been mentioned in footnote[2] on page 194 and it might be as well to emphasise that, throughout this book, the definition of architecture given in the *Concise Oxford Dictionary* as "style of building" is the one in use. There are, however, other terms which may cause some misunderstanding if they are not fully explained, and the chief of these is "townscape" itself.

It is interesting to compare the uses of the word "townscape" in the work of those geographers and architects who have studied towns. Professor Smailes talks of the "urban scene as a townscape, a tract of landscape distinct from its rural surroundings",[4] and he expands this idea of the word as expressive of large areas of scenery, irrespective of their qualities as urban environment by saying that the geographer, in studying townscape, "ought not to follow a conventional literary and aesthetic pattern in apportioning attention to successive phases of urban development . . ." and "would do well to remember that . . . geography is . . . an anatomical study of the content of regions of the earth's surface, with emphasis on those features that invest regions with their essential distinctiveness."[5] This kind of definition is quite different from the one implicit in *Townscape* by Mr. Gordon Cullen. Here we read that if we "bring buildings together . . . collectively they can give pleasure that none can give separately", and "One building standing alone in the countryside is experienced as a work of architecture, but bring half a dozen buildings together and an art other than architecture is made possible".[6] Obviously the townscape, as defined here, is something to be viewed critically, perhaps to be condemned if it is bad, but, much more to the point—for Mr. Cullen is a constructive critic—to be enjoyed to the last detail when it is good (for example, see his illustrations and description of an instance of what he calls "serial vision" in fig. 9).

Fig. 9. "Serial vision" in townscape (after Gordon Cullen)
"The sequence in New Delhi (read the photographs from
left to right) emphasises the role of levels and screening in
serial vision, for here what could simply have been one
picture reproduced four times, each view enlarging the
centre of the previous view and bringing us near to the
terminal building, turns out to be four separate and unique
views"

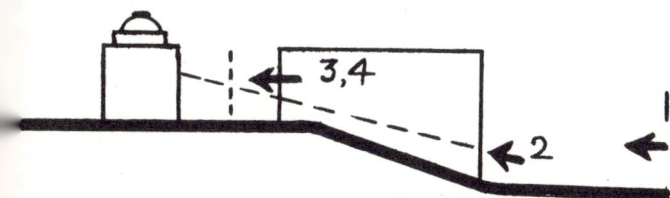

Here then are two views of townscape, which at first sight seem very different from one another. The geographical view is a wide, all-embracing analytical view; it calls for a comprehensive look at the town's scenery—good, bad and indifferent— to help us to understand how our visual surroundings have come about and how they have acquired individuality. The other view is an extension of traditional architectural thinking, claiming for townscaping the place of an applied art, and pointing to its major role in the creation of a worth-while urban life. Although these two definitions are clearly differentiated, and, taken merely as definitions of a word, they are irreconcilable, there is surely no reason why the two ways of looking at the scenery of towns which they express should not be made to work together towards a common goal. A geographer made aware of the qualities of good townscape, in Mr. Cullen's sense, and conscious of the fact that, to-day, changes of enormous scale are occurring at great speed in our towns and cities, may well feel the need to try to bridge the gap that at present generally separates those who are interested primarily in the aesthetic appeal of buildings, and those who see buildings primarily as end- products of the complex actions of society. In the last resort, buildings—either indi- vidually or in groups—must be designed by someone, however complex or simple the design may be. That someone will express, in the shapes he makes in the urban landscape, the accumulated ideas of what a building should look like, as they have been passed down to him through successive layers of taste. It is the intention in this book to consider how these layers of taste have left their mark upon our British towns; to hint at ways in which these might become the subject of geographical analysis; to suggest that aesthetically most periods have both good and bad con- tained within them, and to assert that, at the present time, few aspects of the study of the town are more urgent than those which increase the awareness in students, and in the general public, of the immense heritage of varied character and unex- pected beauty that is hidden behind the grime and the street signs, and beyond the limits set by the guide-book list of "buildings of architectural and historical interest". The word townscape, then, in this book, is primarily used in the geo- grapher's sense of a wide scenic view of a town or parts of a town with common characteristics of design: but the purpose of the study is to help foster the aesthetic enjoyment of our urban surroundings.[7]

There are some other terms, used from time to time, which need explanation, and these have been dealt with as they appear, but some mention should be made, at this point, of the words "Classical" and "Romantic" which are explained in Chapter 2. In that chapter are described the characteristics of what are called the Classical and the Romantic townscapes—two terms which occur throughout the description of the changing styles of buildings and town-plans in Britain. Classical and Romantic, as they are used here, are very closely associated with the two very broad themes which, as is well known, have influenced the course of architecture (and the course of literature, painting and music) in Western Europe throughout most of historic time. But, as will be seen, they are terms which have been given rather more precise meaning as they relate to the various phases of the British townscape, and, in spite of their many associations, and the fact that, like much terminology used in studies of this kind of subject, they are not ideal, they are the best that can be found in the present circumstances.

A final word should be added to this introductory chapter, on the scope and form of the book. The particular examples of townscapes that are given in the following pages are all in existence at the time of going to press.[8] Owing to the speed with which redevelopment is taking place, there may be a few instances where a piece of a town, described here, will have disappeared, or will be much altered, by the time the text reaches the reader, but it is hoped that such instances will be rare. It is no part of the present study to try to reconstruct past townscapes, and particular care has been taken, in the case of early periods of town-design, to choose places where a considerable part of a town is still standing.

The arrangement of chapters in an historical sequence is explained by the convenience of the method, not because this book makes any claim to be history. *British Townscapes* can be seen either as a geographical approach to an architectural subject, or as a study of architectural influences on the geography of towns: in either event it tries to explain an aspect of the appearance of towns as we find them to-day—that aspect which is the product of the impulse to design urban scenery.

2. The National Townscape

Is there such a thing as a national tradition in town design? More particularly is there, to paraphrase Nikolaus Pevsner,[1] a recognisable "Britishness" in British towns?

The habits of a people contending with their environment will obviously lead to plans and shapes of buildings, separately or in groups, that have their own peculiar outlines, textures and colours. Town scenes throughout the world are evolved from either native materials or newly-adopted ones which become a part of the place's own individuality. These materials are worked into the house-forms suitable for the needs of each distinctive social pattern. Furthermore, the artistic instincts of each society are in direct operation throughout a process which is less purely functional than is sometimes supposed. Each house adds to a pattern of houses, each district to a pattern of districts, so leading ultimately to a complete urban sculpture.

When we make comparisons of towns on a world scale we find obvious distinctions of size, luxury and substance. One need go no further than the comparative size and richness of buildings and their various materials to illustrate the existence of broad contrasts. Thus, as Pierre George shows,[2] in the African sectors of Dakar, the characteristic village shapes of thatched wattle huts in asymmetric groups were marshalled by colonial planners into gridiron layouts. The small squarish plots fenced with reeds, stakes, wooden boards, anything to hand, filled rapidly with the typical cone-roofed huts. The geometric forms were quickly lost as, within each tiny compound, the expanding families built more and yet more huts in random positions, first probably peripheral, but soon almost filling the whole space (fig. 10). Finally, a crowded scene emerges of poor little dwellings rising a little above head height. Wattle, boards, beaten tin cans, old mats, adobe, and even occasionally masonry and tiles, hold up the ubiquitous shaggy thatch which, often renewed and tilted to ever-crazier angles, dominates the primitive town-scene.

Contrast this for scale and riches with the towns of North America. Here Lewis Mumford's "Baroque City"[3] has gone far beyond its milder European prototypes of the eighteenth century. These were highly formalised in their central areas, but elsewhere had much of the informality of medieval towns. Not so San Francisco, for example: the great expanse of this urban space has the size and shape which result from a sort of galloping affluence. As in many other American cities, the wide streets and well-spaced building-blocks have the chess-board regularity of the colonial garrisons of ancient Rome. The tentacles of the freeway system add a pattern of unrelated curves, slung and looped through the city, like an emergency respiratory system hastily assembled (fig. 11). Apart from these roads, a rigidly

Fig. 10. Dakar

Fig. 11. San Francisco

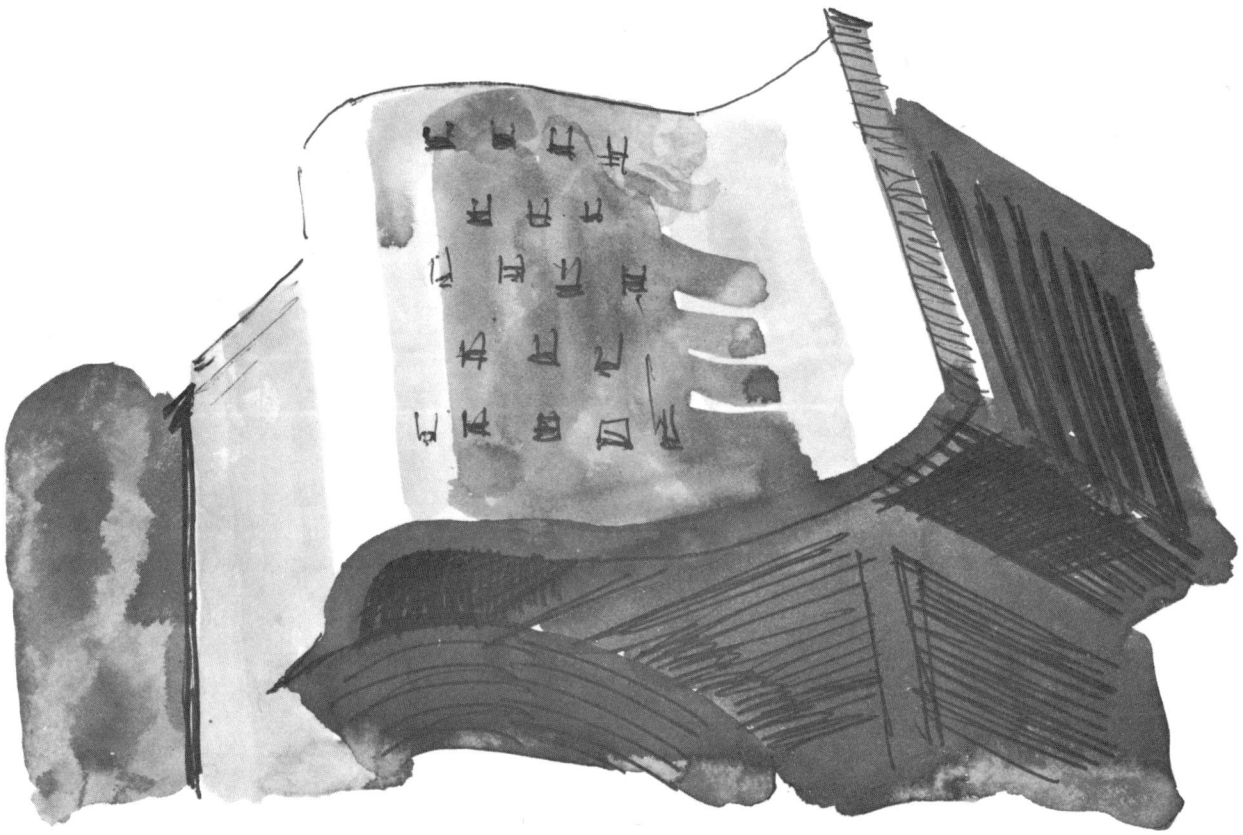

Fig. 12.
Two modern structures
(a) Cardboard factory,
Fors, north of
Stockholm
(b) Part of the
Palazzetto dello
Sport, Rome

Fig. 13. A typical Japanese city (from *Japan* by Glenn Trewartha, after Edward S. Morse, *Japanese Homes and their Surroundings*)
Fig. 14. A part of Auckland, New Zealand

rectilinear form, vertical in the "downtown" zone, horizontal in the suburbs, is everywhere the natural result of producing living-space in a hurry, with no expense spared, out of steel adapted for maximum strength. It is true that girders, or rods—sometimes forming the backbone of poured concrete—can be modelled into almost any shape, as the architecture of many modern structures shows (fig. 12), but these examples demand the added luxury of design for design's sake: in the bustling North American town, first impressions suggest that growth has been simple, regular and repetitive rather than multiform.

The almost featureless indigenous Japanese city is described by Glenn Trewartha (fig. 13). Partly of grid form, but with amorphous accretions, the city street-plan is lined with dull, grey-roofed timber houses. The wood is unpainted, the shapes are of the utmost simplicity. Gently-pitched roofs cover the box-shaped homes. No tree or taller building breaks a skyline of one or, at the most, two-storied buildings.

When a more sophisticated and less land-hungry people sets about planning the urban scene, something like parts of Auckland, New Zealand, may result (fig. 14). Here traditions from the opposite side of the globe have inspired a reproduction of the English village, on an altogether more opulent scale. Trees are encouraged everywhere; the streets are coaxed into the naturally dignified forms of country roads. The houses, of varied design, scale and materials, derive in style from a European heritage as far back as the Renaissance, and even farther.

So, over a world scene of cities, though some aspects of site and plan are ubiquitous, the ultimate townscapes are as varied as the peoples who make them. And as
it may be claimed that European culture and society have the richest variety of any,
so European towns and cities have perhaps as great a diversity of shape as those in
the rest of the continents put together.

Paralleled by the major racial groups, though as intermixed as they, are three
main types of European townscape. Two of these are found in the strongly-con-
trasted towns of the Mediterranean and of Northern Europe. The urban landscape
of the first is boldly exposed, calm and clear-cut; that of the second, "protected",
vigorous and involved. The former, too, has a straight, horizontal "line"; the latter
an irregular, vertical one. Between these, in the Alpine and neighbouring parts of
Central Europe, is a third very important land of towns which bear strong marks of
the other two traditions. Here the firm line of southern building is softened with
elegant calligraphy, while the tougher energetic quality of the north is made more
tender and restful.

These urban properties are the properties of whole layers of European history.
Greece and Rome founded towns with the logic that pervaded their civilisations,
and designed buildings with a corresponding artistic geometry. This tradition
spread far beyond the Mediterranean, mainly by way of the metamorphosis of the
Renaissance. Major building groups throughout the world stem from here, but in
Southern Europe the whole town expresses the incisiveness that was Greece and the
boldness that was Rome. The traditions in design which are generally referred to by
the term Classical are found here not only in the temples and the forums of the
ancients, and in the palaces and churches of the fifteenth and sixteenth centuries,
but also in traditional domestic buildings and in modern hotels. The town on the
shores of the Aegean or Adriatic or in the hills of the Apennines may be termed a
Classical town, and town elements largely derived from it will be referred to in this
book as Classical townscapes (fig. 15).

Northern towns on the other hand are of another species. Product of an indus-
trious struggle to trade and manufacture in inhospitable regions, these places rise
from their plains or low hill-sites like organic growths. Lacking the unification of a
Roman civilisation, here priest and trader have separately opposed powerful prince.
From this three-cornered struggle has come a political preference—democracy—
and an architectural one—the Romantic style.[4] The tall, narrow, steep-gabled
houses and the soaring Gothic church-forms seem to epitomise northern indepen-
dence, rectitude and spirited compromise: they combine to make the Romantic
townscape (fig. 16), as urban areas of this type will be called throughout this study.

Fig. 15. Frosinone, south-east
of Rome

Fig. 16. Edinburgh
—the old town

Fig. 17. Prague from Charles Bridge

Fig. 18. Florence from the south

In some parts of the mountains of Central Europe are towns with the vertical lines of the Gothic, but of more delicate build. These form the "fairy-tale" towns-capes of Switzerland and southern Germany. But elsewhere, nearer the centre of past empire, the splendours inherited from great ruling houses and a dominant Church have led to the rich building style of Austria and her neighbours. The luxuriant late harvest of the Renaissance in these areas is perhaps the high-water mark of the European architectural image, from which the Baroque townscape has been produced (fig. 17).

We shall now look a little more closely at examples of these three town styles. As a source of European town-building tradition, perhaps no other place compares with Florence. In its greater buildings it stands for the purest elements in the rebirth of the ancient language of architecture; in its whole townscape, also, it possesses Classical attributes. The city, seen from across the Arno (fig. 18), is dominated by those two great features—the Cathedral, with its famous dome (half-Gothic, half-Roman) and the tower of the Civic Hall, in which the stern lines of the fortress give way to an almost spire-like delicacy in the upper parts. But it is to neither of these two major architectural "highlights" that the city owes its characteristic shape. The rest of the town refuses to soar, and, in spite of the many tall buildings jostling on the crowded site, the long, low-pitched roofs make an insistent pattern of horizon-tals, and those buildings which can be distinguished separately are all of the most carefully considered proportions, and the placing of their every window, doorway, arch and column gives expression to a delight in logic and symmetry.

The Baroque town is a unique contribution to the main stream of urban design. There is a refined intimacy in the morphology of this town style that is best illustrated by such a scene as that of the Maria-Theresien-Strasse at Innsbruck (fig. 19). Here the nobility of the mountain backcloth is matched by the scale of the street and the height of the dignified buildings that line it. Although these buildings have a core of classical symmetry, not one has failed to add to the composition its quota of delicate embellishment. First, the roof-line above the splendid cornices is rich in domed turret, gable and dormer. Then some of the façades carry rising columns of bay windows, capped with little canopies, each with successful variants in the pattern of their glazing bars. Other frontages in more uniform style stress the well-placed lines of rectangular windows, or the groups of round, arched ones, with firm incision and unfailing success. Even the shop signs and street-furniture (overhead wires and all) seem to fit into this picture of an environment of completely committed urbanism. Thus the most successful of the Baroque townscapes have cast Italy into a new and rarefied mould.

A final example from the three main forms of European urban design may be found in Middelburg in southern Holland (fig. 20). The contrast between the shapes of the central area of this Dutch town and those of Florence is eloquently proclaimed by the tall, sharply-ridged house-tops of the former place which give the townscape a fretted and irregular profile and a vertical "thrust", so different from the elegantly prone posture of the Italian city. Most of the fronts of the shops in the square at Middelburg have, of course, been altered since the building of the medieval structures which form the chief part of the scene behind the façades. These fronts are the exception to the general rule that, in this northern Romantic town, the "natural" tendency is to design within the limits set by the irregular thoroughfares and house-plots. By making a virtue of necessity an overall composition has been achieved, by balance and not by symmetry, and it is the particular rather than the general which has been cultivated in this delightful town, of friendly appearance, scaled to human needs.

How has Britain received and modulated the continental townscape? What is to be said of the native British town style, if there is one? In most sectors of the field of design, Britain has always been an integral part of European trends. Her byword insularity is often only an extension of what is to be expected at the periphery of a continent. If one is looking for similarities rather than differences, there are very few shapes in building or in town-plans that cannot be shown to have some connection with those of Europe. Many such shapes have extremely precise derivations, as in the various uses of the Greek "orders" on the façades of large buildings copied from the innovators of the Renaissance. If differences are being sought, however, then the persistence of certain features, even if copied, suggests at least peculiarities of taste; while other details like the colour of materials, or the skylines created by the characteristic chimney-pot, are the direct result of a singular economy, society and environment.

The question with which we began this chapter may now be restated: are our townscapes indigenous or borrowed? Is there a native approach to urban design which has received much from outside but which is still recognisable? Or is there only a European town which has been given a British look? If by "indigenous" we

Fig. 19. Maria-Theresien Strasse, Innsbruck

Fig. 20. Middelburg, south Holland

Fig. 21. Main-road housing
in the present century

mean only "of purely native origin", then clearly no answer can be given in the present state of knowledge, since we can point to no "original British town". But if we take the *Oxford Dictionary*'s definition of the word, namely "native, belonging naturally" we have a wider brief. What is truly British in the appearance of a town is not what is left of its beginnings, but what has survived in it that is different from towns elsewhere. We may mistake the most historic for the most genuine. It takes the fires of time and change to test really intrinsic qualities. This interpretation is the more justified in the present context, since our theme concerns the town *to-day*.

Many studies of the geographical characteristics of towns have been confined to the explanation of street-plans, building-plots, and other urban characteristics which are emphasised by maps. But if we are concerned with the design of buildings it is necessary to lift our eyes from these records to the street and town scenes around us now. Then we are shown that Britain, though at the receiving end of much imported style, is on balance a part of North European tradition in building. Further, these islands have their own native variant on this regional style. Where Classical design is concerned—and half our major public buildings and much besides are in this vein—there is a clear debt to Italy and Greece. But where the Romantic in our towns and cities is in question, that "romance" is British; it is home-bred. Altered Netherlands and German styles are often found, it is true—for instance in mansard roofs and tall stepped-gable fronts—but these are foreigners and can be spotted immediately.

What then are the characteristics of British town landscapes? Is the individuality nothing more than can be expressed in such a description as—frame and plaster from the past, and chimneys from the Industrial Revolution? After all, the towns of every European nation can be reduced on analysis to a conglomerate of box-like buildings with pitched roofs, flat or bay windows, arches, towers, and spires, and with streets and open spaces between them; but the variations in scale, style and grouping of these components add up to something unique to each country. British restraint likes roofs that are steep but not "too" steep; fairly big but not very big windows; some but not "too much" ornamentation, and gardens which screen the untidier bits of the premises but do not prevent the neighbours from seeing how well ordered the frontages are. In general design it is the same—a cunning compromise. To take the gardens again: symmetry and formality rarely dominate completely, but neither does the Romantic or the "naturalistic" layout. In houses, irregularly-placed windows and doors "elbow" the regular ones, and often win the day. Perhaps the best place for getting a true picture of British taste in these matters is in the average privately-built suburban estate, or along the ribbon-built main

roads on the outskirts of towns. Here the whims of builder and buyer have had free rein (fig. 21).

The lines of the historic townscape show the same thing: the irregular early Tudor is followed by the increasingly formal Elizabethan, the symmetrical "Queen Anne"[5] and Georgian by the riskier balance of the "Regency" and early Victorian; the neo-Classic parallels the neo-Gothic in the mid-nineteenth century, and at the present time the "garden-city picturesque" vies with building of geometric simplicity.

Within the context of British architectural styles there are also conjunctions of the Classical and the Romantic. The "Queen Anne" style, for example, for all its severity and symmetry below the level of the eaves, has the high-pitched roof, the tall brick chimneys, and sometimes the gabled dormers of the "rising" Gothic fashion. Our town character emerges from many compromises: it is near to, but could never be confused with, that of its European neighbours. A British town can seem more secretive and less clean than wide-eyed honest Amsterdam; more humble than proud Burgos; less stern than reserved, defensive Stockholm; less delicate than the sensitive and mannered towns of Austria, and neither so horizontal as the towns of Greece nor so vertical as those of southern Germany. In the plan of streets, the grouping of buildings and the design of individual structures, British towns are restrained and somewhat uncommitted, but the final flavour is of a Romanticism periodically formalised, not of a Classicism sometimes Romanticised. Even modern town-building (which must use so much architectural form of the international "cubist"[6] type) is, in Britain, beginning to show a preference for irregular layouts and grouping—for example in the street and pedestrian-way plan of central Coventry, and the massing of buildings at the Bull Ring in Birmingham. In thus choosing to plan the informal it may be that, through its architectural expressions, Britain declares itself, though truly urban, not excessively urbane.

The object of later chapters in this book will be to describe, historically, the main elements of design surviving in British towns. It may therefore be appropriate to conclude the present chapter with an example of a British town of very modest size, which is representative of what is general in the national townscape and also contains within itself a fair cross-section of period styles.

Dawlish, a small town on the south Devon coast, is inhabited by about 7,000 people and occupies a rather restricted valley site. It is a modern town in that its development, beyond the scale of a very small village, dates from the early years of the nineteenth century. Thereafter, growth has been steady but very modest, no one phase of building having outbalanced the others in the final composition. The

Fig. 22. Dawlish, Devon, from the north-east

demand for seaside holidays, over the last century and a half, has never produced an explosive period of expansion in Dawlish, owing to the limited opportunities presented by the physical site for the kind of amenities that the larger English seaside resort provides. However, its excellent beaches and communications have ensured a steady growth, and there has been favourable reception for each new wave of architectural fashion.

The central area of Dawlish is quite different from that of many older English towns: it does not contain a defensive site, nor is it formed from an original nucleus around a church or town hall. These latter are, in fact, on the outskirts of the town in the upper part of the occupied valley. The centre of the town is in the section of the valley floor nearest the sea, and the rest of the building rises, from here, up the steep sides of the narrow trough, and spills out along the cliff-top, especially on the north-eastern side (fig. 22). In the valley part, which was mostly built-up by the beginning of the twentieth century, stuccoed buildings predominate and preserve the tradition begun by the ancient cob-walled[7] cottages. Elsewhere there has been an increasing intrusion of brick into the scene. Although a good deal of important building dates from the "Regency" and early Victorian periods, and is based on Renaissance formulae, the first impression is of an informal townscape.

While it would be impossible to justify the choice of any town to represent all that is typical of Britain, Dawlish can be shown to possess, within a small compass, practically all the major "period-elements" of town scenery. There are a few small glimpses of late-medieval cottage-groups, and there are contemporary private estates: between these is a continuous succession of building styles. In general, of course, Dawlish experienced the smaller outer ripples caused by the constant stirring of the pot of architectural taste, and scale is muted by the limitations of cost in

24

a small Devonshire town. But on the other hand, any seaside town must count modishness a part of its economic life-blood and so, though remote, this little resort contains examples of many styles.

Confined by the valley of Dawlish Water, and gradually linking two older settlements, one inland, the other almost on the shore, Dawlish grew in the nineteenth century into a long valley-town. The old village straggled on a well-drained terrace on the south-facing slope of the valley opposite the church. A few cottages stood near the stream, and a few clustered by the church itself. To-day, the narrow street pattern in these parts, the disposition of the buildings, and the character of some of the façades help to retain the late-medieval image—irregular and picturesque.

The old "town" was separated, by meadows and cultivation, from a group of fishermen's cottages near the beach, until about 1800, when small houses in the Georgian style began to appear at the sea front and along the valley between the two ancient settlements. Soon afterwards, in 1810, a scheme to lay out The Lawn, and to encourage building developments in the growing resort, was started by John Edye Manning, who had acquired land in the lower part of the valley of Dawlish Water. Many of the buildings of this time have disappeared, or have since been completely altered, but some remain with additions which have not wholly disfigured them. Enough is still there for central Dawlish to be described as a small townscape, of late Classical type, but restrained, and completely devoid of the pomp of the metropolitan style (fig. 23). The buildings in this period are mostly low and give a fairly horizontal line. The mid-nineteenth-century "contest" of Classical and Romantic styles only reached Dawlish at rather domestic level and the Classical came out an easy winner at first. A liking for stucco with Classical details, even occasionally Baroque ones, has given much of the character to the admittedly polymorphic sea front, while Italianate villas are found on the best sites overlooking the town and beaches. The retention of stucco meant that there was real continuity in the texture and colour of the town, though generally bigger and bulkier-looking structures spread from the "Regency" nucleus. The most striking of these are the early-to-mid-Victorian terraces and villas, where the proportions are very similar to those of the preceding period, e.g. Haldon Terrace, Plantation Terrace, East Cliff Road, and some of the buildings facing the upper part of The Lawn. In the third quarter of the century groups of houses in Barton and Longlands were added; these, like the previous ones, chose spacious and elevated sites on the successive terraces of the valley. Cottage-building proceeded at the same time and a good deal of the land in the lower levels of the valley still lying open, between the old town and the sea, was filled in by such streets as Brook Street.

From about 1880 to 1910, building was considerable, and of a style that must have seemed revolutionary to the townspeople of the time. The multi-coloured, multi-textured buildings, both public and private, of this phase, draw short, straight lines on the maps, and bring variegated brick and dressed stone into the town scene. The larger buildings, especially the branch banks, occupy key corner sites or positions of importance in the main street-compositions, and play a part out of all proportion to their individual size in the whole townscape. Equally dramatic must

Fig. 23. Dawlish, the central area

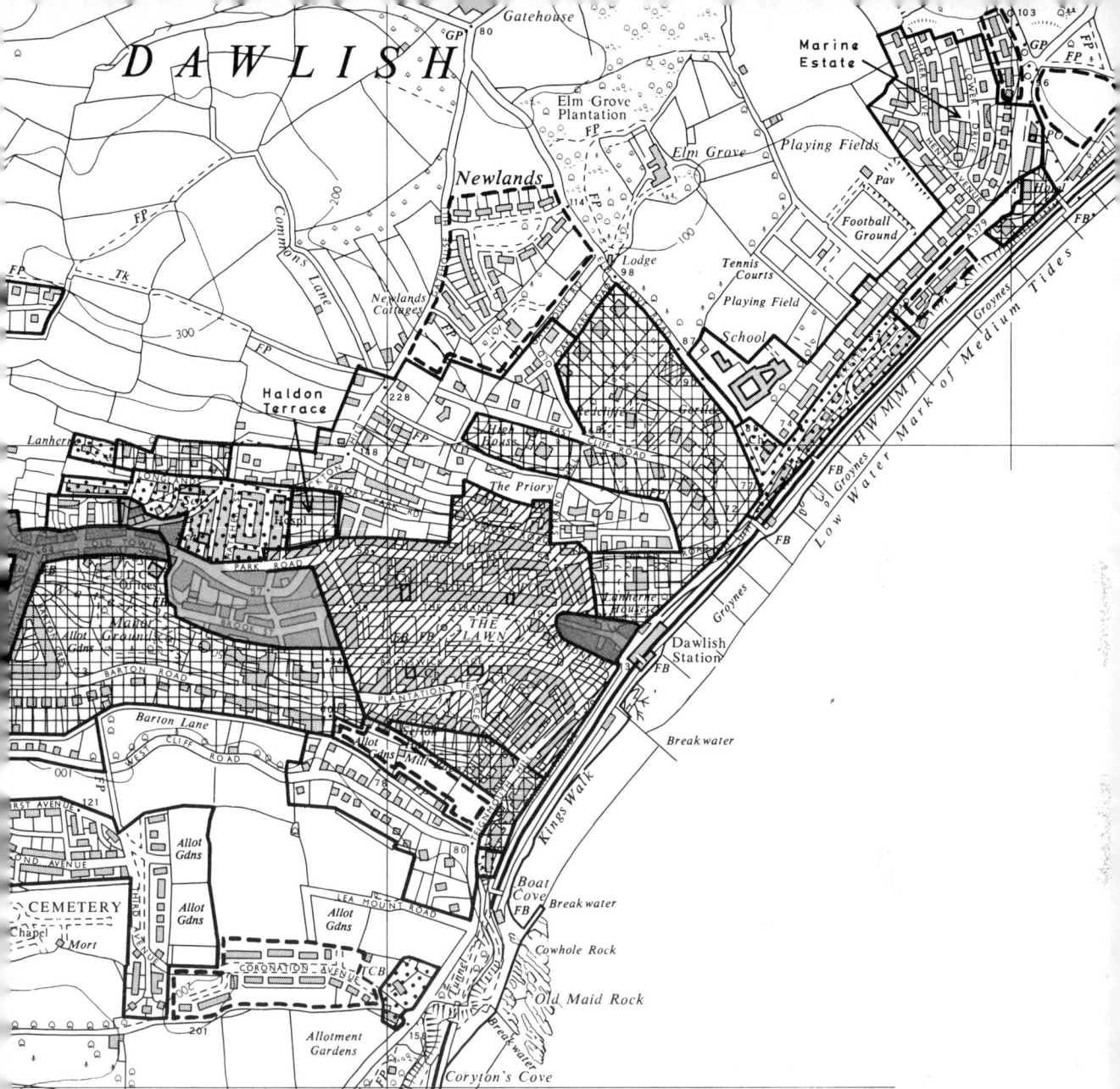

Fig. 24. A map of building-styles in Dawlish
(adapted from O.S. 6″ to mile, 1963)

APPROXIMATE DISTRIBUTION OF
BUILDINGS BY PERIODS

Before 1800

1800–1825

1825–1880 (mainly villas)

1825–1880 (mainly cottages)

1880–1914

1914–1945

1945–1960

have seemed the recasting of the mould of the main shopping-street of the older part of the town, Park Road, and the erection of the uncompromising red-brick terraces behind it. The whole period is more vertical in the accent of lines, and mixes Classical with Romantic feeling—the first below, and the second above, the line of the eaves.

The Garden City Movement had its long-distant repercussions in the style of private building, of various qualities, between the two world wars; this was chiefly at West Cliff and at Marine Estate, and in the small groups of residences near Stockton Hill. West Cliff has some good examples of individually-designed picturesque villas of contrived irregularity and Tudor flavour. Marine Estate, on the other hand, has all the characteristics of ribbon building on suburban main roads (described by Osbert Lancaster as "By-pass Variegated"—a phrase that might almost be adopted as serious terminology) with the minor variations of styling outweighed by the uniformity of scale, regularity of spacing, and inflexibility of building-lines. Of the same period is the first council-house building in First, Second and Third Avenue; this has a more utilitarian version of the garden-estate than is found in West Cliff, but a more picturesque end-product than the Marine Estate building. The whole of this phase uses stucco again, frequently in the rough-casting of sections of façade and in combination with some brick construction. It also swings the total townscape more decidedly towards the Romantic.

Finally, the Second World War and the post-war building phases have, in council and private estate, moved very cautiously into the territory of modern architecture, with many backward looks and some "eyebrow-raising" importations, like the mock-Spanish villas of Teignmouth Hill. Contrary to a prevailing idea that modern methods and materials necessarily cast the contemporary town into a uniform and universal mould, this latest period has, if anything, greater variety than almost any preceding one, owing partly to a native uncertainty about adopting new ideas. This most recent phase has thus contributed yet again to an intricate compound that is characteristic of British towns and which is illustrated in the map (fig. 24).

Dawlish, of course, is more representative of the south of England than of the north of Scotland, and more of the residential country town than of the industrial city. It has, too, some distinctly regional undertones that will be discussed further in the next chapter. This small town does, however, argue much for the element of compromise in the British townscape. The irregular impositions of the "Regency" on the more formal Georgian; the Romantic garden layouts added to symmetrically designed Victorian villas; the Gothic upper quarters of terraces of Baroque formalism; and finally the tentative execution of "garden village" layouts in the little private estates of modern bungalows—all these are examples of the mixing of elements which can be found on an extensive scale in our larger towns and cities. The impression that finally emerges is unforceful, organic, and conglomerated. It is picturesque, too. It is well studded with trees, warm in stucco and unaggressive brick, and it leans, in spite of many Classical features, towards the qualities of the Romantic townscape.

3. *The Region and the Town*

THE principal part of this book will be concerned with the forms, surviving in the present urban landscape, which are representative of various historic phases of building style. A separate volume could easily be devoted to the way in which the period styles themselves have been affected by regional practices. Just as there is a national townscape, so too is there a regional one, and this chapter is intended to indicate briefly some of the ways in which the appearance of town scenes, of various ages, is diversified throughout the length and breadth of the country. Of course regional variation is itself due to conditions which are fundamental to the full understanding of all town-building activities—conditions, that is to say, of economy, society and habitat—but a consideration of these things, in any detail, would be to depart from the main theme of this study. But some mention of these matters will help to place the factor of design in relationship to other factors also affecting the look of towns. The importance to the whole urban scene of, say, the swing in taste from the low-pitched roofs and flat façades of Georgian times to the steeper pitches and the bay-windowed fronts of the late nineteenth century, should be seen against the background of such things as land-use practice, and land prices—which help to dictate the position, size and shape of building-plots and to explain how they vary in different parts of a town or city as well as from region to region.[1] Even more, so far as regional appearances are concerned, the availability of good stone for building; the need for protection (locally) against severe climatic conditions; the relief of the ground on which a town is sited—and many other aspects of physical environment—may be borne in mind, as a cause of local variation, even if first place is to be given to the part played by the main periods of design in the shaping of townscapes.

Before the Industrial Revolution, regional character in towns was abundantly expressed in the nature of the building materials used in both humble domestic structures and the notable public and other principal buildings. The difficulty of transporting heavy building-stones or other substances any great distance, before good roads or railways existed, meant that only on rare occasions (such as the erection of cathedrals, palaces, castles or great houses) could an area afford to import materials considered to be of a superior nature to the ones close at hand.[2] For this

29

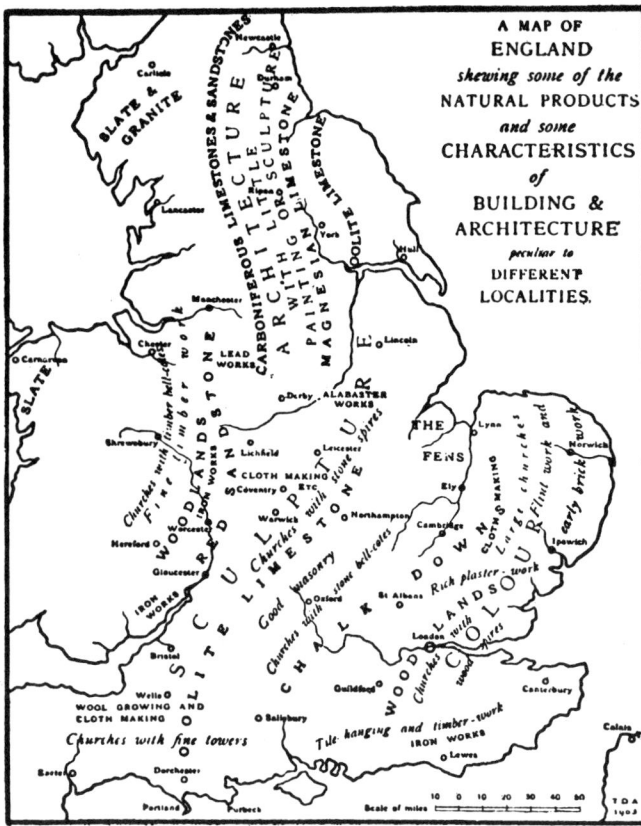

Fig. 25. A map of building materials
(after J. D. Atkinson)

reason, settlements sited on extensive vales of clay, covered for the most part with forest, had houses built of a framework of hewn oak trunks, with the spaces between the beams and uprights filled with woven twigs, or laths of inferior wood, and covered with a mud plaster. In mountain or moorland regions, where there was plenty of stone of a kind (though often it was heavy, rough, angular slate or coarse, intractable granite) and usually a sparse supply of timber, small stone houses were built of irregularly shaped lumps of rock. More fortunate areas possessed freestone —that is, stone which lends itself naturally to being squared-up for building purposes—and these, particularly in the limestone belt from Portland to the Humber, contain some of the finest church and domestic architecture in Britain.

The geological map of this country was, therefore, at one time a safe guide to the general appearance of towns and villages. In his *English Architecture*, J. D. Atkinson illustrates the range of the influences exerted by materials on the principal shapes and colours of buildings, and shows how the detail, decoration and surface texture of houses and churches are marked evidence of regionalism (fig. 25). Now this map is, in the first place, very generalised. It cannot show the multitude of further local variations in constructional substances that make a journey through parts of many English counties a pictorial lesson in economic geology; in the second place, it is necessarily a most inadequate picture of the extent to which this type of regional differentiation has survived in towns and cities down to the present day. It is primarily in the villages of Britain that there are still to be seen—reflected in walls and roofs—the local rocks, soils and natural vegetation. But, although most large towns have lost extensive areas which were originally constructed consistently in a regional material, many such zones still exist (fig. 26), while a surprisingly large number of small towns retain a strikingly unique appearance resulting from a long history of utilisation of local resources.

Fig. 26. The attractive local brick of Golden Court, Hampstead

Some instances of this sort of thing may be quoted. Atkinson's map, concerned as it is with relating building material to our finer works of architecture, cannot show the enormous regional variety that exists in the colour and proportion of the humble brick. The various shades of grey and yellow in the eighteenth- and early nineteenth-century buildings of London, for instance, result from the colour and constitution of the clays which were worked in a multitude of brick-fields around the old city. John Summerson points out that the choice of these bricks depended on changing fashion, and that, just as the red bricks of Queen Anne's time were superseded by the grey ones of the mid-eighteenth century, so these, in turn, gave way to others of a pale yellowish-brown in the later seventeen-hundreds.[3] In this instance it can be seen that choice between various local materials was made according to current modes of taste, and this is true in the use of brick throughout the country and throughout the whole history of house-building to some extent; nevertheless, there are always some limits set by what is available, at the price builders are willing to pay, and it is then that the conditions of nature may impose their terms. While the metropolis was able to afford, from time to time, to change its view of what it thought proper in the colour of its bricks, it was still limited in its choice to those colours produced by the deposits of the lower Thames valley. Again an ochre-coloured brick, with markings of reddish-brown, is found in the York area, and a rusty-red brick is used for the Georgian buildings of Exeter. In both of these cases the local clays are responsible for the prevailing colour. Industrial towns in the West Midlands have dark-red brick terraces giving on to pavements of blue-black tiles, Scarborough has houses of pale yellow, Leicester's bricks are salmon-coloured, Manchester's are brown, and throughout the country the shades of red, brown, grey and yellow in our brick buildings are almost as numerous as are the towns in which they appear.

Stone, of course, imposes its own character on buildings, and sometimes on a whole town. Cornwall has towns built almost exclusively of stone from that county, including slate and shale, granite and other volcanic and metamorphic rocks. The granite in particular gives a yellowish-grey appearance to the places where it is widely adopted, and its hard, rough surface—which makes the mason's task of working it, in any detail, difficult if not impossible—helps to limit the contrasting effects of period styles. The cottages of miners, quarry-workers and fishermen look much the same whether they were built in the seventeenth, eighteenth or nineteenth centuries. The later ones are generally taller than their predecessors, and the stone in them is usually more precisely cut, but the granite will allow few liberties to be taken with its natural form, and the local climate discourages the making of structural additions in other materials, since these might be removed by strong gales, or rotted by the attack of persistent rains. Even the late nineteenth-century houses of Penzance, displaying as they do the bay windows and steep roofs associated with the style of the times, have yet, in the overriding character imparted by their grey stone walls, some affinity with the cottages, farms and churches of early Cornwall.

The settlements of the Cotswolds, especially Bath, contain some of our most beautiful townscapes as a result of the attractions of the oolitic limestones as building material; and less well-known, but not less comely, towns have arisen in Dorset, Wiltshire, Oxfordshire, Northamptonshire, Lincolnshire and Yorkshire on geological outcrops of a similar type. In North Wales hard, dark slate gives a feeling of rugged angularity to buildings, while in the West Riding of Yorkshire a host of small towns seem to be hewn, in their entirety, from the native millstone grit (figs. 27 and 28). And so one may continue to describe the picture of stone-built towns or town areas—in South and Central Wales, in the Lake District and the Border Country, and throughout Scotland.

Fig. 27. Howarth, Yorkshire, from the churchyard

Fig. 28. Howarth, the main street

Close investigation of an area will often show that, although it has no one substance exclusively employed in its buildings, there is a range of materials which together add up to something unique. For example, a region consisting of soft, crumbly breccia (a naturally concreted rock made of small fragments) may use it for the side and back walls of buildings in its towns, or face it with stucco, while importing—from, say, up to fifty or so miles away—a good sandstone or limestone for house fronts, quoins or other corner-stones, lintels, sills, etc.; roofs may be of tiles, and garden walls and outhouses perhaps of rounded cobbles which have been obtained cheaply from neighbouring river or beach deposits. This kind of mixture may be replaced in another area by a good local brick as the common material for house fronts, while shaly rock or something like the rather soft Lias limestone is perhaps used for the less prominent walls and plot-divisions; blue slate for roofs, and bright red tiles as decoration in suitable places may complete the common style. Some parts of the country are within easy reach of varied geological resources and it is these which will tend to have a composite picture. Summarising a very complex situation it may be said that, in traditional building, the very far west and the very far east of Britain are, in general, limited to one or two "earth materials"—hard crystalline stone in the former area, and clay (with occasional flint or chalk) in the latter—while in a wide and irregular "belt" of England, running from Devon to the North Riding of Yorkshire, a wider range of geological conditions has given richer rewards to the search for things with which to build.

An example of a type of townscape with a variety of building materials in it is provided by the outlying districts of many towns in South Lancashire. Here, although so much of the central parts of towns is composed of brick, there are many other materials which are employed with brick to make up the general picture. From the underlying Carboniferous system of rocks, the Flagstones[4] provide a fine building material which survives in most of the early domestic construction, as well as in a good deal of building of later date. In its native state the stone is the colour of pale honey with some brownish stains in it, and this is often darkened by coal-dust, though not to such a dense blackness as covers the other kind of millstone grit of the West Riding. The Flagstones appear in a variety of forms, and are used differently at different periods of building history. They may make a dry-stone wall in a garden, or be cut into regular brick-like shapes for the outside walls of houses. They are common in the older houses not only in the walls, but in lintels, door-pillars, sills and even roofs—where the thinnest of the bands of this rock are employed instead of slates. They are also found in use as paving-stones, as blocks or "sets" for roads, and, carved into troughs, as gutters for rain-water. They "reappear", after a spell of building in brick, as a common material in late Victorian times when "rustication" became popular, and in buildings of this period they often form the façade only of an otherwise brick building. Cobbles—rounded stones derived from a variety of geological sources, and obtained from the extensive boulder-clay deposits of the region—are also found in very old walls and pavements, though they are not a common sight, but brick is, of course, very frequent in occurrence. This is made from local clays and varies from a fairly dark brown to pale yellow, with a medium-brown colour as the most common one. It is not unusual to see slate-hanging on the weather side of terraces or individual houses, but this is usually done with imported Welsh slate, which is the material most in use for the roofs of the brick houses, and which, together with the occasional orange-red glazed bricks (also imported) of some fairly modern buildings, completes the list of principal materials used in this area.

Even greater variety of means is employed for building construction in south Devon and an example of this is to be found in the town of Dawlish, referred to in the last chapter. The area around the lower part of the River Exe is short of a good building-stone (although occasional lumps of sandstone and breccia of the Permian series are found to be hard enough to use for "rubble walls") and so the traditional method for wall-building was cob. This "earth" material was normally in use for the farmhouses, cottages, barns and garden walls in this area up to the nineteenth century, and such buildings were roofed with thatch. In the last one hundred and fifty years or so, the hard Devonian limestones, from Torbay, have been introduced into the region and may now be regarded as almost traditional materials. They are a very light grey colour with a stain of pink, and are either exposed to view or are covered with stucco, as the style of the time of building has dictated. There are rich red bricks in the area also, and yellow ones from the nearby clays of the Bovey Basin. Cobbles, including flint from the Haldon Hills and a variety of beach pebbles, are very frequently found in garden or outhouse walls, and the habit of "roofing" both cob and limestone walls with pantiles is a very distinctive characteristic. Altogether it can be seen that the profusion of geological sources available in this part of Devon has direct reflection on the townscape.

Sometimes the materials from which a town is built make an immediate impression on a newcomer; at other times the site of a place is much more remarkable than are any of its constructional details (fig. 29). Maps and descriptions—especially those which classify towns in groups related to function or size—leave us with but the scantiest idea of the real atmosphere or "feel" of the place. On seeing a town for the first time, however, its general shape from a distance—or even its lack of one, if it is on monotonously flat land—is a factor of the utmost importance in forming a lasting impression. There are towns on hills and towns in deep valleys; towns on hill-sides and in saddles or basins; towns on cliffs or around harbours; towns where a wide river cuts decisive shapes into the urban form; there are towns on gentle, undulating plains and others on spurs of high ground from where they dominate the plain below. It is possible to look down at Truro and up at Durham, and to do both to parts of Edinburgh; Glasgow comes alive—as London does—at its river bank; Birmingham is built on low hills, but points from which it is possible to view its general form are infrequent; Bristol lies in a great bowl; at Liverpool the extensive flank of the hill facing the great estuary dominates all other impressions of the city, while at Cardiff there is no site of any dramatic consequence and the fine civic buildings are a compensation for the rather dull River Taff and its duller alluvial plain. In reality every town is noticeably, and often strikingly, different from every other town. Although ports can be lumped together as towns with some common characteristics, and market centres can likewise be classified, no one port is very much like another, because of the immense variation in the features of coast-

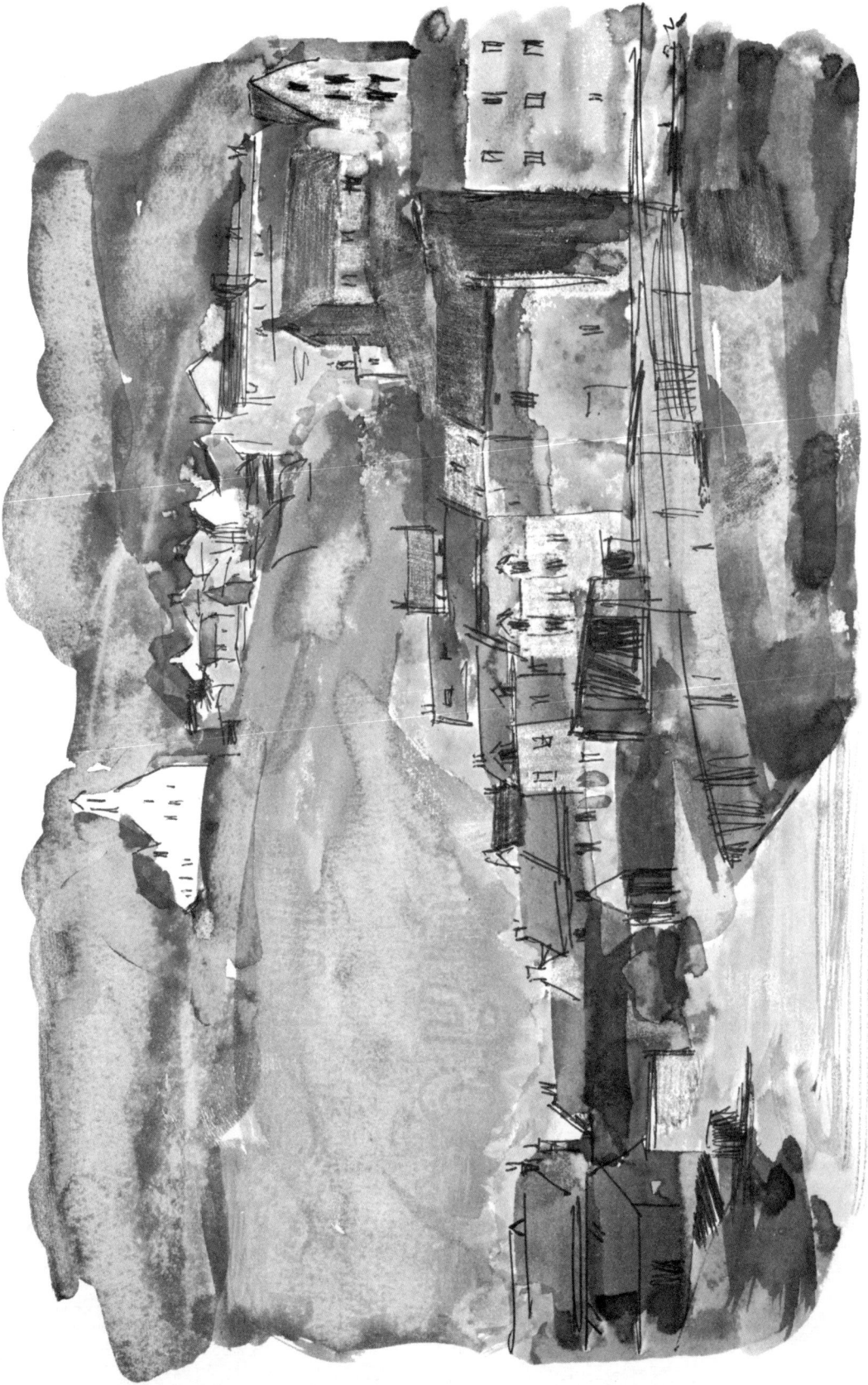

Fig. 29. Gardenstown, Banffshire, climbs on a Scottish hillside

Fig. 30. The Town Hall, Dunfermline

Fig. 31. Hall-i-the-wood, Bolton

Fig. 32. Houses, Falkirk

lines; and market towns, although, perhaps, a little more alike than ports are, all have unique sites, however subtle the differences may be. Thus the detail of the shape of the ground chosen by the original settlers in a place, which by now may have been completely lost to view below the houses and streets, is ever present in the ultimate urban form, and, in spite of the changing styles of roof, chimney, steeple and tower, the major features of a town's profile are those of the ground beneath its feet.

So far it has been shown that local conditions may modify a prevailing style. But style itself can also be a product of local conditions and, from small beginnings, can become of wide-ranging significance. The development of local style in building is so closely linked with the use of local materials that, in most cases, it is virtually impossible to separate the two as factors in producing the town landscape. Local style, moreover, in its strongest expressions, has long disappeared from the principal urban scenes and been replaced by national, and even international, traditions; but on close inspection it may still be seen that builders and designers are following some local custom in the handling of stone or in the choice of a site, and there certainly remain some significant townscapes that depend for their character on the exertion of some regional preference. The cause of this character is not always easy to find. Is, for instance, the enjoyment of height in buildings something which the Scots derive from their mountainous country, or is it linked with their own physical dimensions? The tendency to construct tall buildings is, without doubt, partly a legacy of times when the needs of defence demanded the construction of fortified houses. But all mountainous areas, and most countries, have been through a period of fortified building without necessarily retaining a tradition of tall buildings. In Scotland the impression that every house is made with one or two more stories than a similar structure in England (where the shortage of building space is just as severe, perhaps severer) is very powerful indeed. Here, then, is one way in which a sense of style strong enough to affect the whole urban appearance has developed, perhaps from some originally functional shape. The feeling of height in Scottish building is especially emphasised by the frequency of occurrence of the turret-shape, a form which derives from the traditional "tower-houses", now, of course, obsolete. These turrets, especially the type sometimes known as "pepper-pot", are described by W. Douglas Simpson, who says that "the roofed-in turret with its pointed helmet forms a charming element in the picturesque skyline of our later Scottish castellated mansions".[5] He could have added "and of our towns", for, as the view of Dunfermline Town Hall shows (fig. 30), the Scottish town scene can be dominated by similar shapes.

Traditional building methods in England reveal, on close inspection, a multitude of styles which local craftsmen have learnt and handed on. In areas like the West Midlands, East Anglia and Kent, all of which once depended on timber and plaster, with occasional local stone, and where from the sixteenth century onwards brick steadily replaced the plaster, there are regional differences of style which cannot be explained except as expressions of a native instinct for making designs with constructional materials. The towns and villages of Lancashire and Cheshire, for instance, used the bold lines of timber framework to make square-shaped patterns, and sometimes superimposed on this base elaborate, even, some may say, burdensome decorations (fig. 31) which have powerfully influenced much domestic building in the twentieth century: in Suffolk, on the other hand, wooden-frame buildings are much more restrained in the use of decorative devices, while in Kent weather-boarding and tile-hanging to cover plaster surfaces are common. These traditions are not just confined to a few ancient villages. Although probably little is known of the extent to which suburban building takes its forms from local style, there is ground for supposing that there is such a connection. The Midlands in general seem even more addicted to half-timbering, in the building of the nineteen-twenties and thirties, than do most other parts of Britain; the South-East still likes the hip-roofs and weather-boarding of Kent; and, to take an illustration from beyond the regions of this immediate discussion, stonework has continued, during the present century, to be enjoyed in many parts of eastern and northern England as well as in Scotland (e.g. the road of semi-detached houses and bungalows in Falkirk, fig. 32). Again methods of laying bricks, by means of Dutch, English or other "bonds", may have some regional distribution.

Some details of regional practice have little general effect on townscapes to-day. The custom of colour-washing the stone cottages in Pembrokeshire, like the making of raised patterns in plaster (known as pargetting) in East Anglia, are dying tradi-tions and are only found in isolated instances. Thatching styles vary from place to place, and ways of giving to stone a rusticated or other decorative surface depend, to some extent, on the local stonemason's whims, but do not, of course, have a big impact on towns. A good illustration of how an old method of working—which originated in the conditions imposed on a builder by the peculiarities of a particular medium—can be translated into a style which is enjoyed for its own sake is provided in the "brick areas" and described by A. K. Wickham. Speaking of the half-timber construction of many parts of England, he says, "Originally the spaces between the timber in such buildings were filled with wattle and plaster; later . . . brick began to take its place, but the timber remained, although it was no longer necessary. Such brick filling of timber framework is known as brick nogging, and nothing illustrates better the conservatism of the old English builders. Even when their material changed, they saw no reason to alter their style".[6]

To what extent regionalism is still a significant factor in the design of town-scapes it is very difficult to say. Throughout the present century, writers on archi-tectural matters have stressed the uniformity of style that has been imposed by the blanket adoption of mass-produced substances, a process that has been assisted by the ever increasing efficiency of transport. And yet this seems to be an oversimplifi-cation of the position. Yellow bricks are appearing again in modern buildings in London, and granite chimney-breasts are built into contemporary bungalows in Cornwall. Common style and common materials were in existence at least by the eighteenth century, and Georgian proportion, Renaissance detail, and stucco are a mixed bag of abstract and material elements which are common to buildings from Cornwall to Caithness. In every period, even in the most provincial corners of Britain, there has been some aping of the fashions of the metropolis, and, through these, of European trends also. To-day there are far more building materials more easily available than ever before, but it is wrong to assume that all regional indivi-duality has been lost.

4. Late-Medieval Town Scenes

ALTHOUGH there were many towns in medieval Britain, they were generally much inferior to their European counterparts. Congested, irregular, primitive hut-like buildings clustered around the few larger houses of the well-to-do, and formed a lumpish contrast to the elegant lines of the church or cathedral (fig. 33). This state of affairs continued up to the end of the fifteenth century. Thatched houses, often built on supports of wood, were regularly damaged by fire, and as congestion increased, so did the severity of these fires. The one which destroyed much of central Warwick in 1694 is an example of the sort of disaster which, like the Great Fire of London, obliterated the old scenes and forced comprehensive rebuilding projects in many towns. The new building took on styles of marked contrast with what had gone before, since taste had meanwhile caught up, though belatedly, with the Classical Revival that had already swept Italy and France. In many towns, even those with long histories and traditions dating back to the first charter in Norman days, there are only very scanty survivals of complete late-medieval buildings, and nothing but sketchy relics of anything earlier. Although in a few English towns one can still see a substantially complete medieval street—as in The Shambles at York —nowhere, perhaps, does there exist an extensive survival of what may truly be called a medieval townscape.

In Britain the "Medieval Town", apart from its historic meaning, is thus a mystique existing only in the minds of people whose winter-evening dreams are inspired by the quaint village street on the calendar over the "mantel". The mystique, however, is none the less important for being nothing more. It is this very image of a bygone, intimate urban prospect, irregular, picturesque and "homey", that has activated the designers of much domestic building ever since. This "old world" vision probably still constitutes the ideal of the average Briton, passed down through the "toy-town" scenes of popular art and literature, and is in sharp contrast to the imported, modish, urban designs derived from the Italian cities. There has been an unbroken tradition, at least in the provincial towns and villages of Britain, of a picturesque style. Right down to the nineteenth century, domestic building was sometimes untouched by Italian influence, while from the middle of the eighteenth century the revival of Tudor and Gothic shapes was converting the

Fig. 33. Coventry: part of a painting by an unknown artist, probably about mid-eighteenth century

forms of the Middle Ages into something more sophisticated (fig. 34);[1] this latter trend was, moreover, followed quickly enough at the outset of the twentieth century by the Garden City Movement which also championed the earlier styles. The high place accorded to the eighteenth century by historians of British architecture has done much to divert our attention from our instinctive preference for a Romantic town picture. Although the complete medieval town scene is veiled from us, many of our county capitals, and some other smaller towns (often referred to as "historic"), can be said to have a strong medieval flavour. Many altered town centres have retained medieval qualities because the process of change has been largely superficial. It is true that if fire damage, the ravages of war, or the processes of decay were extensive, then completely new street-plans were possible. Wider and straighter roads sometimes resulted, and the building-lines followed suit. But often, if destruction or decomposition was slight, only the fronts of buildings became altered with fashion. Then, though new styles of window, doorway and surface material, with appropriate decorative detail, appeared on the new façades, the street-shapes and basic building-structures remained the same. In such cases there is still an urban character of the earlier period which can be defined and analysed.

This character is made up of three main elements. These are, firstly, the plan and shape of the streets; secondly, the outline of the building-plots and the ground-plans of the buildings themselves; and thirdly the form of the buildings, including their decorative details. These three elements may be considered in turn. The meandering narrows of old streets are the most obvious and the most persistent surviving town medievalisms: old town maps may be compared with new ones to show how little has changed in some cases. Cartographic record is scanty before the sixteenth century, however, and, up to the early years of the nineteenth century, it is very inaccurate. The splendid early example of Salisbury is, certainly, well documented, but quite untypical in that it is one of the outstanding examples of medieval town planning in this country; the town has spacious streets in a formal

42

Fig. 34. A romantic eighteenth-century house in Exeter

layout. In the case of Exeter the principal thoroughfares have changed little since at least 1587, when Hogenberg mapped the town. The illustrations (figs. 35 and 36) show Hogenberg's plan, together with a similar portion of the present-day city taken from the Ordnance Survey map at six inches to the mile.[2] Although the scale of the earlier map is inaccurate, the position of the wall (marked in on the modern map), and of the various churches, enables most streets in the central part of Exeter to be identified. These streets have remained substantially unchanged throughout the four hundred years that have passed between the making of the two records, and furthermore we know that this same street-plan existed from at least *circa* 1200.[3] Neither map, however, brings out to the full the unmistakably medieval quality of the street pattern. It is the slight deviation from the absolutely straight line that is important. There are no long vistas, and within the enclosed street scenes the irregular building-lines still occur in places as major features of the urban morphology. Exeter was well laid out and fairly rectilinear in the plan of its streets, though this did not make it formal, geometric or regular in its townscape.

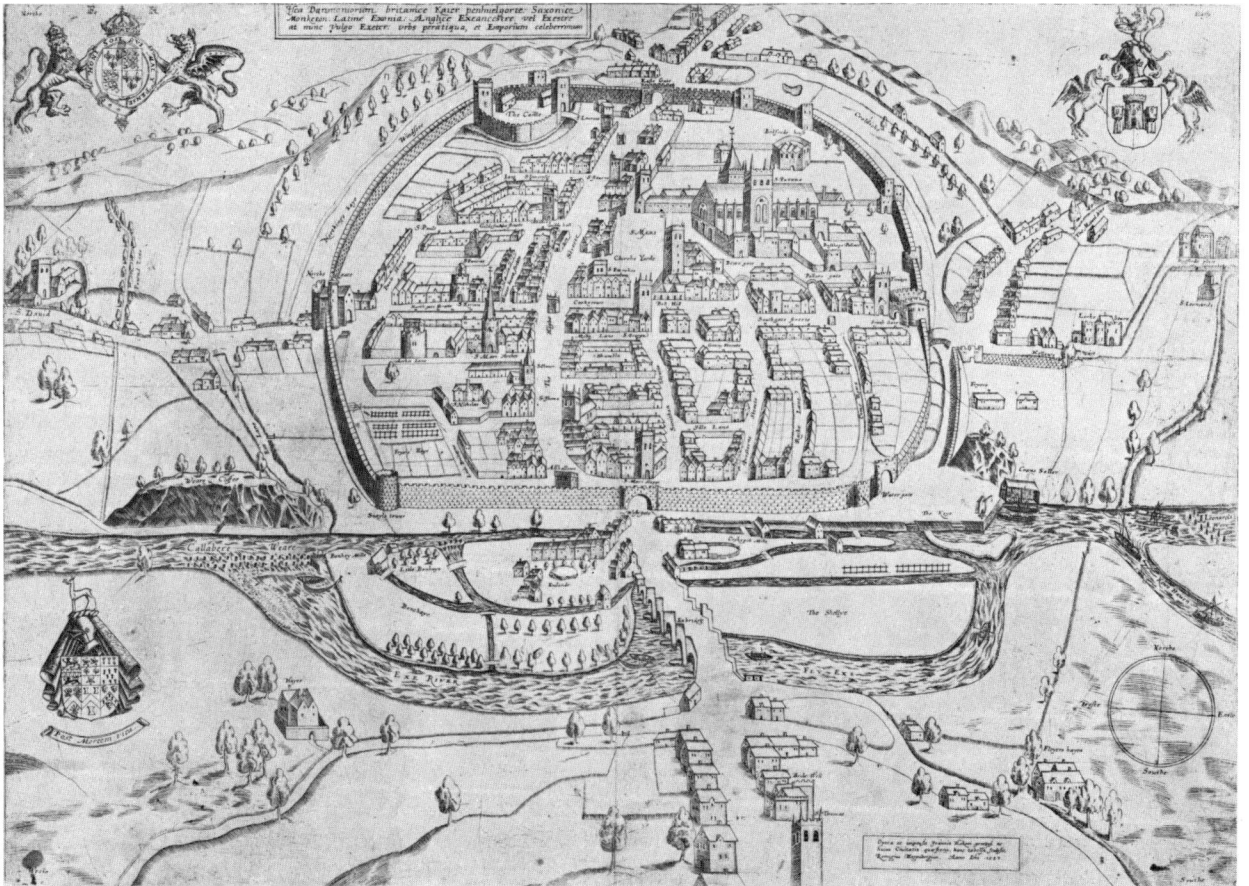

Any townscape, especially when viewed from above the chimney-tops, is also in part the product of the plan of the building-plots. In the medieval period the shape of plots was partly dictated by the lines of ancient fields and tracks, streams, the limits of a lord's estate, and so on, and where these plot-shapes have been preserved and have dictated further accretionary out-building, they are a very important part of the medieval character of towns. The example of Alnwick, Northumberland, has been meticulously studied by M. R. G. Conzen.[4] The part of his work dealing with the medieval town shows that, together with the lines of the old streets which—at the junction of the main arteries at the centre—pre-date Anglian times,[5] there are "plan-units" which are characteristic of the period of growth from the earliest settlement down to the end of the Middle Ages. These plan-units are the plots and building ground-plans in combination. They vary in depth from the road-frontage and are more complex, congested and irregular than any of Conzen's later plan-

Fig. 35. (*opp. page*) A map of Exeter in 1587 by Hogenberg

Fig. 36. The same area of Exeter today. (O.S. 6″ to mile, 1963)

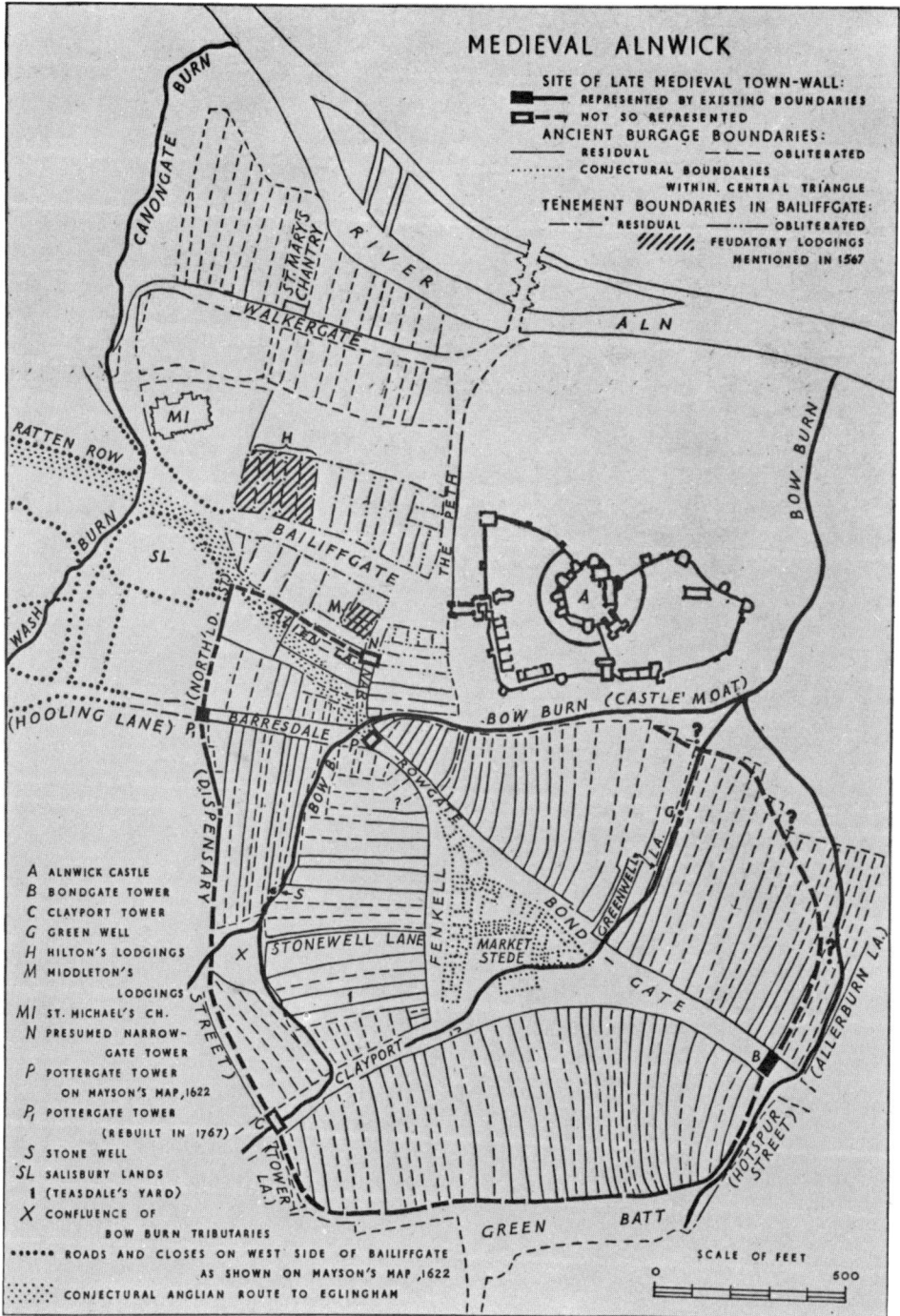

Fig. 37. A map of Medieval Alnwick (after Conzen)

unit divisions. The illustrations (figs. 37 and 38) show how much of central Aln-wick's roof-line pattern and building-shape derives from the plot characteristics, and how these plots are closely related to the ancient burgages, which in turn relate —in their general disposition—to old roads, streams, etc.[6] Streets and plots of the type we have described, the product of hundreds of years of evolution, can hardly be said to be designed, except in the very crudest sense, yet their form is not entirely the result of expediency either, for there was considerable attractiveness in the intimate street and market arrangements, and the best was undoubtedly made of the frontages of the narrow building-plots.

Fig. 38. Alnwick from the air. (The main street in the foreground is the Clayport)

Fig. 39. A view of the Rows at the Cross, Chester

The structure and detail of the buildings of the medieval period, which form the third element of town character, certainly have something more than pure utility. Although hewn oak beams do not lend themselves to the making of straight lines and perfect right-angles, there is every reason to assume that the builder-craftsmen took delight in the patterns formed by their irregular shapes and in the overall shape of the building which arose from these (fig. 39). Medieval buildings which have survived in some of our ancient towns are usually the better houses, shops and warehouses, and these have come to be the touchstone of the medieval urban architecture. But the outlines of many medieval buildings are more persistent than we may think, and a good deal of structure of early date survives, even if in an altered costume. Superficial skins may cover the old forms, like a recent deposit covering a hard band of rock which still gives major shape to a landscape. Examples include cottages clothed in a Georgian or "Regency" covering, which replaces thatch and half-timbering with tile, slate and stucco, with enlarged doors and windows inserted in the face (fig. 40); tall medieval buildings in crowded main streets with masks of Georgian or later date (fig. 41); and the multitude of altered but not completely rebuilt houses and shops lining the streets of older towns particularly in central and southern England.

48

Fig. 40.
A house in
Regent Street,
Dawlish

Fig. 41.
Altered Medieval
façades, York

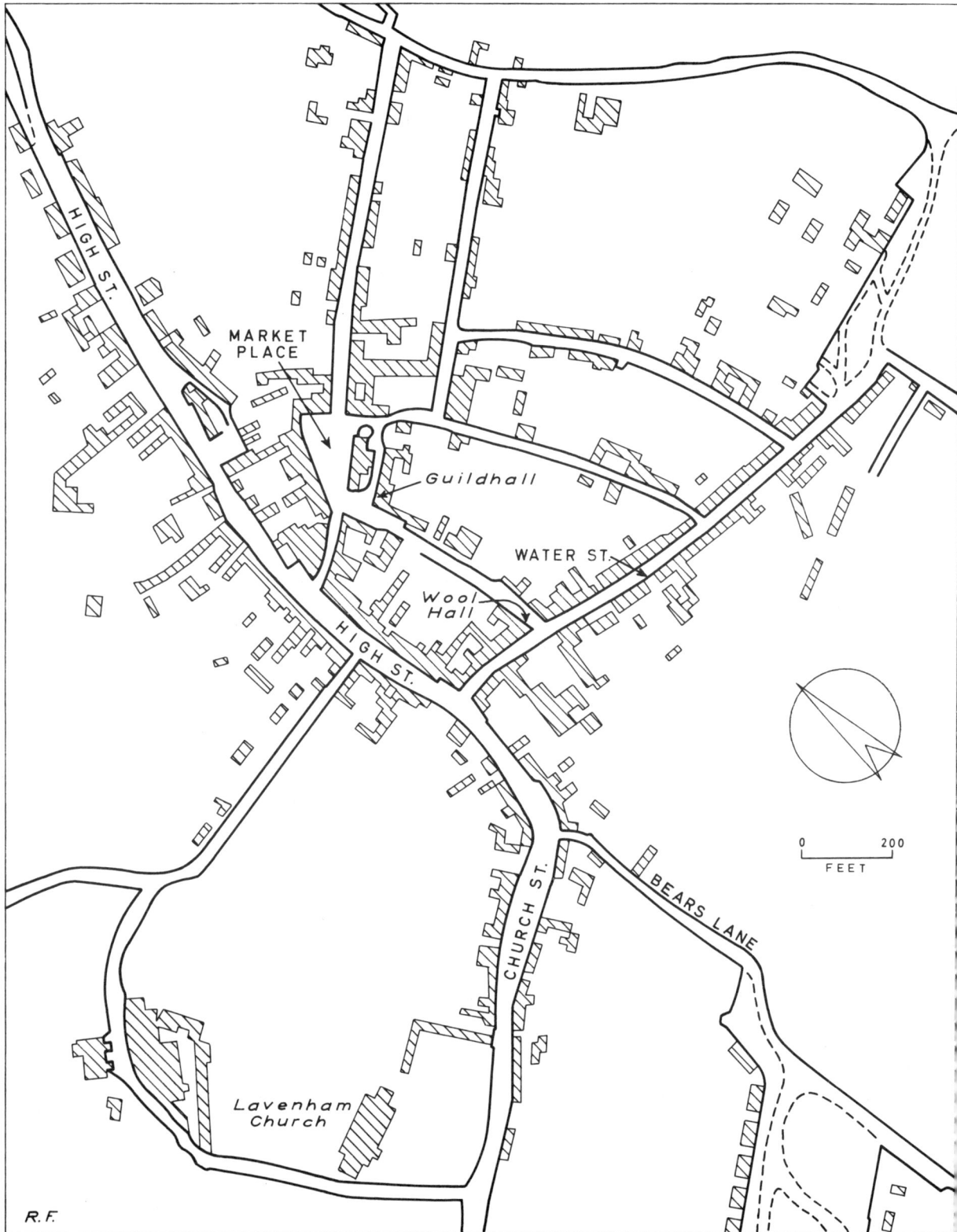

MARKET PLACE

Guildhall

WATER ST.

Wool Hall

HIGH ST.

HIGH ST.

CHURCH ST.

BEARS LANE

Lavenham Church

0   200
FEET

R.F.

Fig. 42. A plan of Lavenham (adapted from O.S. 6″ to mile, 1958)

To find extensive examples of medieval town scenes is difficult. Two principal illustrations will be given, namely, Lavenham and Warwick. The first, Lavenham in Suffolk, was formerly a cloth-making settlement, which reached its peak of wealth in the fifteenth century, and has, perhaps, the most consistent large area of genuine medieval building in Britain. Although its population is only about 1,500 to-day, A. K. Wickham describes it as "perhaps too much of a town" to be used as an example in his book on English villages.[7] Its inclusion here may be justified further on the grounds that larger and more virile towns have no comparable areas surviving from the Middle Ages. The plan of Lavenham is irregular (fig. 42). The main thoroughfare formed by Church Street and High Street wanders down from the church to the bottom of a shallow valley and up the opposite slope. At a very rough right-angle to this, Water Street follows an old stream-course with a meandering gait. In the angle of these two main streets lies the market-place, reached by several link-roads of varying width and direction. The plan-units (to use Conzen's term) show an elongated form in the more built-up parts of Lavenham, reminiscent of the burgage plots of Alnwick, and even perhaps of the shapes of strips in the open field system. The roof-lines in the air photograph (fig. 43) demonstrate this pattern.

Fig. 43. Lavenham from the air, looking south

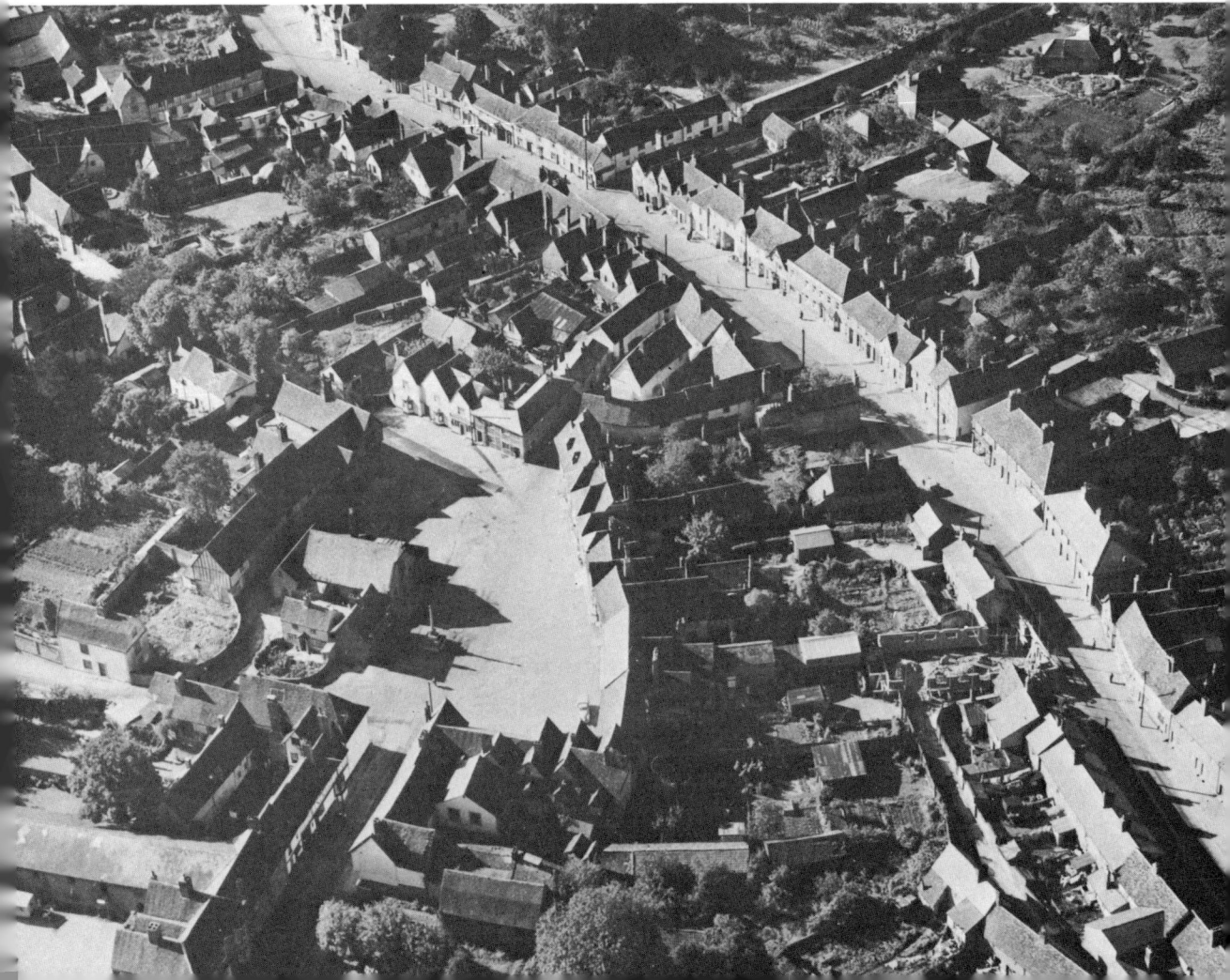

Fig. 44. Church Street, Lavenham, looking north

These roof-lines frequently run at right-angles to the streets, with the result that gable ends face the main thoroughfares and open spaces. In most cases the medieval core in the older British towns contains traces of this arrangement, but very rarely is there such well-developed gable-fronting as in many of the towns of Holland, Belgium and southern Germany. It is in its retention of gables, and of large dormers (where the line of the roofs is parallel to the streets) that Lavenham demonstrates most strongly its medieval character.

The town must be studied at ground level to get the full measure of its design. No survey map or aerial view can reveal the intention of town-builders who lived before such aids to planning existed. From the junction of Church Street and Bear's Lane the most comprehensive ground-level view of Lavenham is obtained (fig. 44). The knarled old town crawls over the low undulations of the Suffolk chalk-lands

like a vegetative growth. Its foundation-garment of oak dictates the characteristic line, which is rugged and "alive". A horizon of sharp peaks is drawn by the angles of the high-pitched roofs. The majority of the buildings are pre-1500 and several are firmly dated well before this. F. Lingard Ranson says "Many of the houses were built before the Wars of the Roses, and most of them during that war".[8] He goes on to date many of the individual houses, e.g. "In Bear's Lane Nos. 87–90 are a block of fifteenth-century buildings" and, in Water Street, the "Flemish Weavers' Cottages, Nos. 23–26, are amongst the very oldest cottages in Lavenham . . . The date of erection . . . is c. 1340".[9] Even where Elizabethan, Queen Anne, Georgian and other frontages occur along the streets, they can easily be shown to cover more ancient structures. The Georgian style never dominates the street scene, but always appears as a minor intrusion.

The morphology of this small town illustrates to perfection the essential elements of the Romantic townscape, which have already been referred to. They may now be summarised as they apply to a medieval settlement. The formal content of Lavenham is made up of irregular street-plan and street widths; erratic building-lines; uneven lines and diverse heights of roofs; amorphous open spaces; the haphazard arrangement of building groups, sections of building façades, and the windows, doors and half-timbering of individual buildings; and an overall tendency towards verticality in the lines of the townscape, produced by exposed timbers, high roof-pitch and tall chimneys. Some of these features are less and less apparent as the medieval period reaches its close. Although the town itself was changing very little, individual buildings were beginning to show the imprint of the precision and formality of Renaissance notions of design. The larger and later timber houses of Lavenham have a measure of symmetry, and straighter and more regular lines than their predecessors (fig. 45). It was by this path that medieval buildings progressed towards the style of the Elizabethan period, which contained a compromise between medieval balance and verticality, and Renaissance symmetry and horizontality. This style was a characteristic compromise, but it has an inherent Romantic streak. (An outstanding case of this compromise is to be seen in the College architecture of Oxford and Cambridge; but as this has been so exhaustively treated elsewhere, and as it produces a highly specialised form of building which is not characteristic of British townscape in general, it need not receive more than a passing mention here.)

How conscious was the designing of a medieval town like Lavenham? Probably very little indeed. Simple carving of the trusty oak was a pleasant frill, and frequent examples of decorative use of materials undoubtedly lie behind the stucco of many frontages to-day. But there is no urban style in Lavenham. Ancient enclosures and lanes must have helped to direct the plan, and occasional community needs were satisfied by the casual open spaces. Building materials and methods were poorly adapted to making sophisticated architectural experiments. The forces at work are epitomised by the explanation given by Ranson of the siting of a group of buildings in the Market Square.[10] These—and others which at one time stood in front of the Guildhall—are successors to ancient market-stalls which "took root" and became permanencies (fig. 43). Many larger towns than Lavenham, e.g. Winchester, Chester or Exeter, all of which had more rectilinear layouts, must nevertheless have looked very much like the Suffolk town for the greater part of the Middle Ages. Odd corners of the Lavenham type of town scene survive still in a multitude of old towns and villages, and these valuable relics of the medieval Romantic townscape have played a part, out of all proportion to their extent, in influencing the design of British towns of later date.

A different but more common type of survival may now be observed in Warwick, which is a good example of the town with long traditions. It has a site of great antiquity and physical importance; a form relating to its early function as a refuge and market; and many scattered buildings and town-relics of great age.

Fig. 45. The Wool Hall, Lavenham

Unlike Lavenham, Warwick has not even one complete street of medieval buildings, but the major modern street-lines are close to those shown on John Speed's map of 1610 (figs. 46 and 47). Stressing continuity, Thomas Kemp claims that the appearance of the town in the sixteenth century (and therefore *before* the great fire) was little different from that in his day.[11] He gives us this description from a study of early sources:

"The main thoroughfares and chief features of Warwick in the sixteenth century were much the same as they are now (*i.e. at the end of the nineteenth century*). Although the great fire of 1694 destroyed a large portion of the town, as well as the nave of St. Mary's Church, there are still enough of the old houses remaining to show us what the Warwick of that day was like. Near to the present Court House in Jury Street, which probably occupies the site of the old one, there stood a cross, which is often referred to as the High Cross, or simply the Cross. If anyone will stand at this spot with his back to the Court House, he will have Church Street and St. Mary's Church facing him; on his right, down Jury Street, he will see one of the old gates of the town, viz. the East Gate, with St. Peter's Chapel above it; on his left, up High Street, called in Elizabeth's day High Pavement, he will see another gate, the West Gate, with St. James's Chapel above it. Both these gateways at the time of the commencement of the Black Book were in a ruinous condition, and most of the town walls were down."[12]

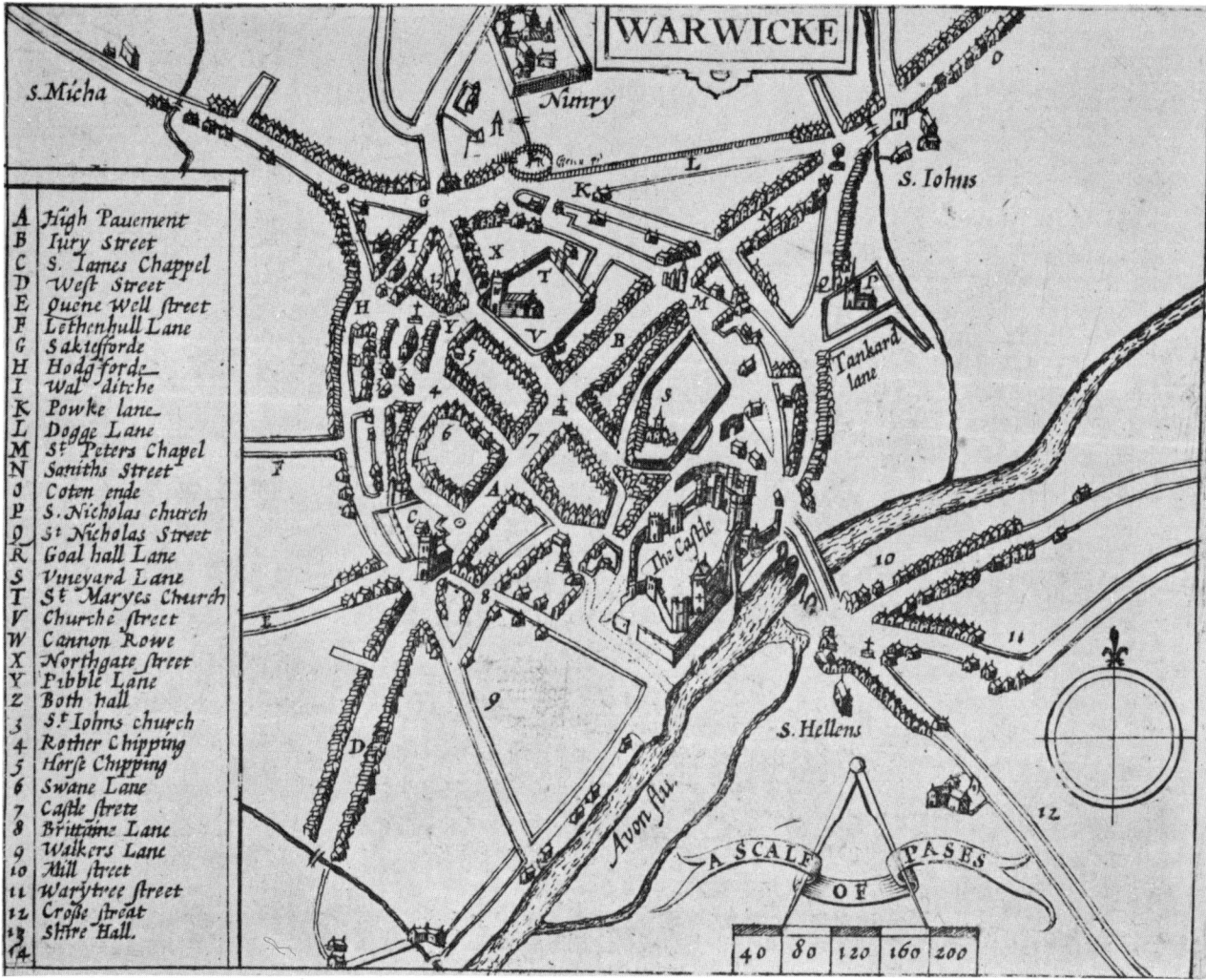

Warwicke

A	High Pauement
B	Iury Street
C	S. Iames Chappel
D	Weſt Street
E	Queene Well ſtreet
F	Lethenhull Lane
G	Sakteforde
H	Hodgforde
I	Wal-ditche
K	Powke lane
L	Dogge Lane
M	St Peters Chapel
N	Smiths Street
O	Coten ende
P	S. Nicholas church
Q	St Nicholas Street
R	Goal hall Lane
S	Vineyard Lane
T	St Maryes Church
V	Churche ſtreet
W	Cannon Rowe
X	Northgate ſtreet
Y	Pibble Lane
Z	Both hall
3	St Iohns church
4	Rother Chipping
5	Horſt Chipping
6	Swane Lane
7	Caſtle ſtrete
8	Brittaine Lane
9	Walkers Lane
10	Mill ſtreet
11	Warytree ſtreet
12	Croſſe ſtreat
13	Shire Hall.
14	

A SCALE OF PASES

40   80   120   160   200

Fig. 46. Inset from John Speed's map of Warwick, 1610

WARWICK

Fig. 47. Central Warwick today (O.S. 6″ to mile, 1955)

Kemp goes on to show that elsewhere the lines of the streets have been little changed, while the major landmarks of the old fortifications dominate the town plan. He admits to some more sweeping alterations, saying that: "In no part of Warwick have there been so many changes as about the old Bridge, consequent on the building of the present bridge, the enlarging of the Castle grounds and the diversion of the road to the Asps, which took place about a hundred years ago",[13] but his main assertion that Warwick's layout is medieval cannot be challenged. Kemp's claim that the main thoroughfares looked much the same in Elizabeth's day as in about 1900 is, however, surely exaggerated. True, the streets in central Warwick are shown as a bold open grid by John Speed in the inset to his County Map of Warwick (fig. 46), but this only suggests that, long before the fire, a simple street scheme, not unlike that of Lavenham, existed. This plan, the earliest known, does not tell us what the buildings looked like, while the street widths are unrelated to any scale. There would certainly not have been a straight building-line like that of present-day Jury Street; periodic widenings and narrowings would have altered the view along the street, and the buildings in oak and wattle would have overhung the pedestrian and perhaps even the waggoner on their way around the town. The shape of the building-plots and the condition of back premises to-day indicate that not all the buildings were totally destroyed by the fire. But "Queen Anne" and Georgian buildings in front of this have altered the townscape, as seen from the street, beyond recognition. The real justification for claiming medieval quality for the Warwick townscape is, therefore, the extent of preserved plots and beheaded building-units which, behind the few main streets, make a genuinely ancient conglomerate of buildings and spaces on sites going back to the sixteenth century and earlier. These can be seen in the air photograph, together with the obviously redesigned main thoroughfares (fig. 48). To-day at street level, however, the centre

Fig. 48. Central Warwick from the air

Fig. 49. Church Street, Warwick

of Warwick is, on balance, not medieval. The destruction by the seventeenth-century fire was great enough to leave most of the town, inside the walls, so altered that it is more a ground for the medieval archaeologist than a surviving medieval townscape. There are a few real glimpses of the old town outside the East and West Gates, and near the Castle where there was less destruction. Smith Street, Mill Street and part of Church Street, though a good deal altered, still retain the essential shapes of the earlier period (fig. 49). Here then, in Warwick, in contrast to Lavenham, we have the more typical scattered remains of the medieval town. As in York, Chester, Norwich and many other towns, much of the real urban appearance from before the year 1500 has been lost. Congestion in narrow streets and evidence in the plan-units of much more ancient occupance is often all we get of an impression of medievalism. But exceptions there are, and some of the famous streets of York, surviving still, provide us with splendid illustrations (fig. 50).

At the same time the town character of these ancient places, which have been much altered by time, is not elegant, formal and grand. They are in no sense Renaissance towns just because so many of their streets have buildings in a Classical idiom. There is an important border country, therefore, between the town landscapes of the Middle Ages and those wholly constructed in the period from about 1600 to 1800. Although in this latter period, as we shall see in the next chapter, there were many outstanding areas of town building in a revolutionary style, it was also a time of steady replacement, alteration and face-lifting, especially in the main streets of the older British towns. At their best the resulting scenes are perhaps our most satisfying contribution to urban design, multiform, durable and humane, and to-day at last, sadly, under the stress of traffic needs, they are dying.

Fig. 50. The Shambles, York

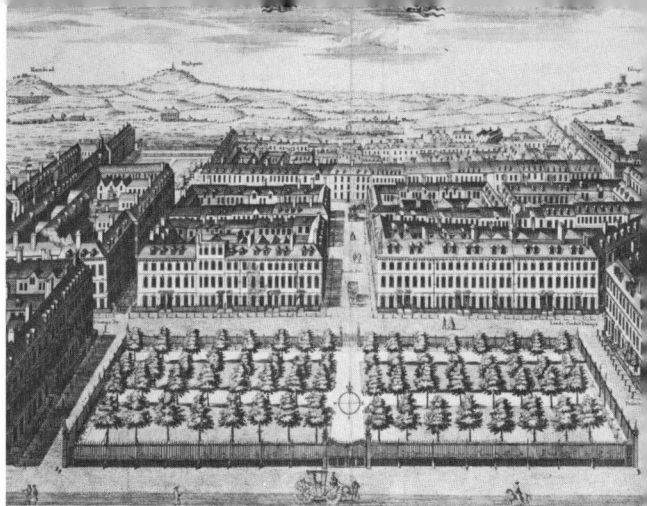

Fig. 51 (a) King's Square, Soho, and (b) Red Lion Square in their original form, from contemporary drawings

5. *The Renaissance in British Townscape*

ROBERT CARRIER and Oliver Dick call eighteenth-century London "The Vanished City".[1] From their collection of magnificent prints of London streets and squares of that period, there emerges a planned town of unbelievable orderliness and rigidity (fig. 51). It is the same with many other parts of Britain; from them, too, has vanished much of the townscape resulting from the influence of the Italian Renaissance. The clean, formal lines of the streets and building-plots of the eighteenth and early nineteenth centuries have sometimes been buried under later building, while elsewhere façades have been redesigned or much softened by the maturing of trees which were once nothing more than straight rows of staked saplings. Nevertheless, the towns of this period have been much more widely preserved than those of the Middle Ages. Though demolition and face-lifting have eaten away large parts of the original urban patterns of Renaissance inspiration, other, and quite extensive parts, still remain. The central areas of some of our chief cities owe much of their shape to this period of planning.

Although new ideas of urban design from Italy and France were making increasing headway in Britain in the seventeenth century, notably through Inigo Jones and the Vitruvian writers,[2] it was not until the early seventeen-hundreds that a major change took place in the morphology of our towns. Since then the characteristics of the change have been amazingly persistent. They dominated urban planning up to the middle of the nineteenth century, and fought a vigorous battle with the Romantic Revival into the early years of the twentieth. The Renaissance tide is even yet casting a few tired waves on the shores of our urban lands. Throughout the country the more pompous bank buildings, to quote but one example, are still mocking the Georgian. Even the modern movement in architecture has harboured a return to English-Renaissance elements: it is common enough to see rows of sash-windows punched into brick walls at regular intervals, next to sections of the same building in modern materials and styles. The "Vitruvian" layout, too, can be traced throughout the twentieth century. Examples are found in civic centres, like that of Cardiff and the very recent one at Plymouth (figs. 53 and 54), and in small residential estates (e.g. Lillington in Warwickshire and at Nottingham figs. 55 and 150).

These illustrations of the power of a style of building to persist for centuries are relevant to the argument that aesthetic considerations are major factors in urban geography. It is the traditional view that the refined beauty of British building in the eighteenth century was the peak of our architectural achievement that has caused us to go on repeating the characteristics of that period for so long. To-day this view is tempered with an awareness of the contrast that originally existed between the fine Georgian houses and the neighbouring overcrowded slums. Now that much eighteenth- and early nineteenth-century building is fighting a battle with redevelopment on the one hand and decay on the other—for instance in parts of Bloomsbury, Paddington, Kensington and Camden Town—we can begin to measure the capacity of this great movement of town-building for survival, together with its significance to British townscape to-day.

Fig. 52. (*See note 2, Ch. 5.*) Palma Nova, north Italy

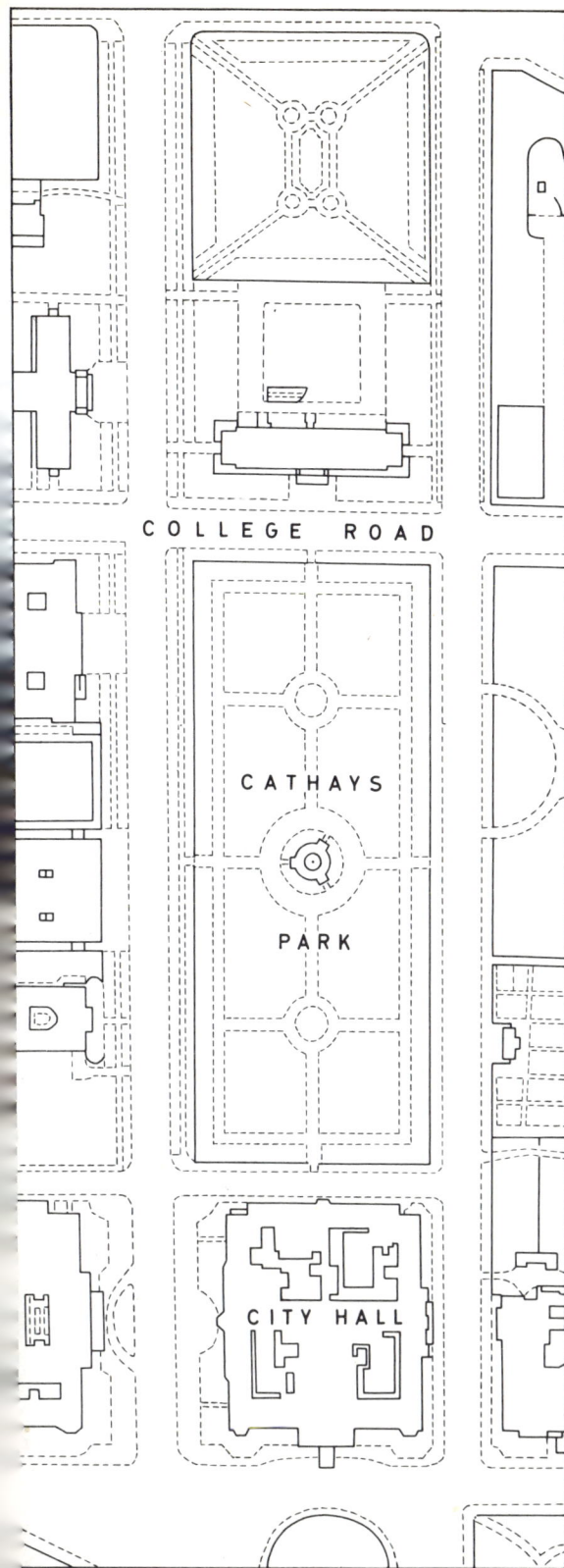

C O L L E G E   R O A D

C A T H A Y S

P A R K

CITY HALL

CARDIFF CIVIC CENTRE

Fig. 53. Cardiff: the Civic Centre (adapted from O.S. 25″ to mile, 1954)

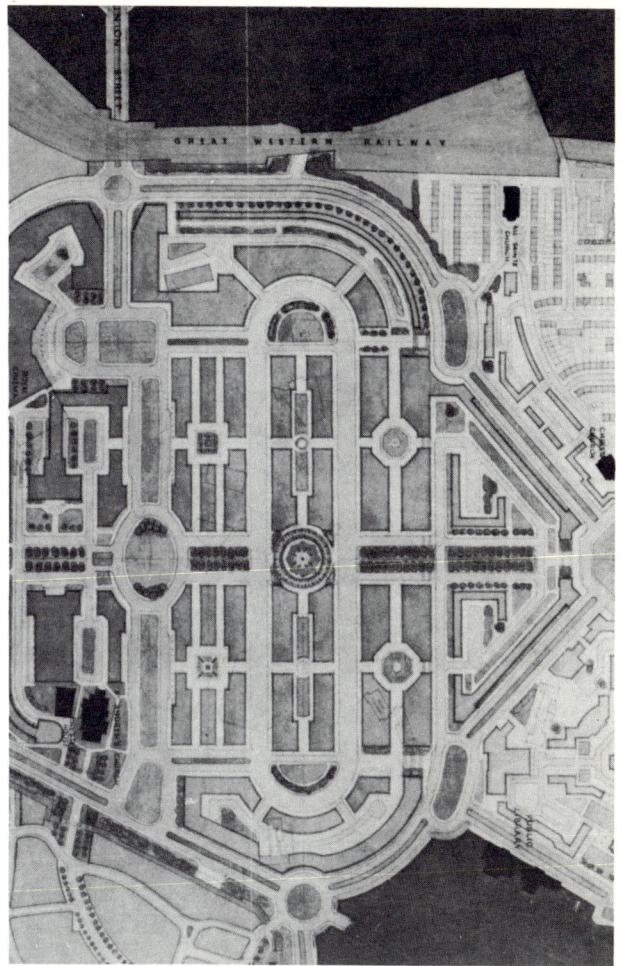

Fig. 54. Part of the central area, Plymouth

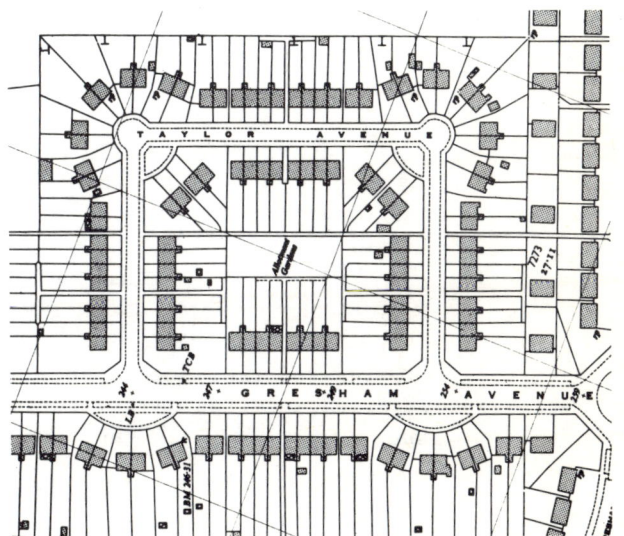

Fig. 55. A housing estate, Lillington, Warwickshire (O.S. 25″ to mile, 1952)

Fig. 56. The Manor House, Blackheath

Architecturally, the house styles of the eighteenth century have been shown to form a climax of an evolutionary process. Tudor and Elizabethan buildings contained Renaissance features, and throughout the seventeenth century there was a steady emergence of the Renaissance town-house. The "Queen Anne" and other styles which thus developed were the immediate heirs to most of the town architecture of the eighteenth century (fig. 56). In town planning terms, however, there was no such steady development (though the laying out of some London squares proceeded in the decades following Inigo Jones's scheme for Covent Garden in 1631). Instead, eighteenth-century town design shows a radical change, both in style and origin, from its medieval predecessor. When the new architectural notions were applied to whole districts, aesthetic values for the first time played a major role in town formation. Earlier towns had grown in conformity with the needs of a rural and trading economy, and planned layouts, though not infrequent, had previously stopped short at elementary street grids. Furthermore the streets themselves were only roughly straight, and the building-line even more irregular. The arrangement of building groups for visual effect and the designing of façades to form homogeneous compositions, with streets, precincts, parks and carriageways as interconnecting space (not only to serve as channels for communication, but also to provide a sculptural element) were startlingly new. Towns were thus transformed in order to satisfy conventions new to Britain since the fall of Rome, but deeply rooted in the European cultural tradition. These were the conventions which had been renewed by the Vitruvian planners and which were to produce the British version of the Classical townscape as distinct from its European parallels described in Chapter 2.

Fig. 57. Barnfield Crescent, Exeter

Fig. 58. The Colosseum, Rome, from the etching by Piranesi

The emphasis on ideal proportion, previously confined to individual buildings, was carried forward in the Renaissance period into the design of whole towns. In Italy, architects like Brunelleschi, and, later, Michelangelo and Bernini, continued the architectural experiments of the early Renaissance and applied them to the piazza and to the building group; as these urban elements were joined up by further skilled "filling in" throughout the principal parts of the city, a whole landscape, informed by the same basic concepts, emerged. This is, essentially, what happened in Florence.

A century or more later, in Britain, the same ideas were being applied to the large cities, spas and resorts; not only to major public buildings and the palaces of princes and aristocrats, but also to the homes of the prosperous, if not fabulously wealthy, middle classes. The characteristics of British Classical townscape result partly therefore from its being built for a large number of moderately wealthy patrons—modest landowners, merchants and new industrialists—rather than for a small number of the excessively rich as, for example, in France and Austria; this no doubt explains the extent and the moderation of its forms. While this social factor in the make-up of towns of the English Renaissance does not invalidate the claim that here was a time when men cared more about what their houses and urban settings looked like than perhaps at any time before or since, it does help to show why designs of the period were still sympathetic to ordinary human conditions.

The best way of defining the main elements of the townscape that emerged from the translation of the urban styles of the Renaissance into British terms is to describe an example. Barnfield Crescent, in Exeter, was built for a prosperous provincial middle-class clientele at the climax of the Classical style in townscape (fig. 57). It is part of the original late eighteenth- and early nineteenth-century grouping of terraces, squares, open spaces and a circus, some of which still remains. It is constructed of warm-coloured brick with string-courses, cornice and window-framing of stone. The gentle curve of the façade is an excellent example of stylish modification which must have involved considerable constructional adjustment (each room is a little "off-square"). Yet this exercise was considered worth-while in order to achieve the resulting elegance. The plan of round-arched lower windows, followed by a succession of well-proportioned smaller ones at each storey, is based on a familiar pattern dating back through Florence to the Colosseum of Imperial Rome. Yet how completely the sense of oppressive power in that ancient arena has been transposed to one of calm freedom (fig. 58)! This subtle piece of town architecture is a fine example of adaptation to the English scale. It has, also, in both design and function, many limitations. The architect has stopped serious operations at the flanks of the crescent, for the sides and the rear of the building are not much more than mere outer walls of the living-quarters behind the façade (fig. 59). The main ingredients of the Classical townscape, as illustrated by this example, are therefore seen to apply to frontal features, and to the views obtained from the main streets, squares and parks of a city. They consist of: good proportions in the largest forms combined with regular spacing of parts; a feeling of horizontality, greatly assisted by low-pitched roofs and masking parapets, and an overall simplicity and cleanness of line.

The Classical townscape in Britain can be divided into two parts. The present chapter will deal chiefly with the eighteenth century, and Chapter 6 will be concerned with the first half of the nineteenth century. The outstanding example of the first stage of the Classical townscape in this country is Bath. The local yellow building-stone has been continuously in use here from Roman times to the present day, and this beautiful material, especially when weathered and a little unwashed, is a consistently fine element in the scenery of the city. The shapes of the buildings

Fig. 59. Rear-view of Barnfield Crescent, Exeter

themselves, emphatically horizontal in the long lines of the terraces, with their stubby chimneys, gently-pitched roofs or low mansards, are characteristically Classical. However, the narrow streets of the old city centre, whose redesigned buildings have been made to conform to the styles of the major planning schemes fringing the ancient nucleus, contain much greater variety of shape than the bold blocks and squares with which they were meant to harmonise. The addition here of bow windows, moulded cornices, and other nineteenth-century features, while creating something quite unique and extraordinarily attractive, prevents the full realisation of the Classical townscape, though this is achieved in the spacious and geometrically planned areas outside the line of the old town walls. The street-plan of the city (fig. 60) shows the chief eighteenth-century layouts to be those from Queen Square to Lansdown Crescent, together with the Bathwick patterns across the river from Pulteney Bridge.

No map, however, could reveal the quality of the Bath townscape, which possesses something very different from the disciplined order of the Vitruvian model. Walter Ison, discussing the planning of the city and the criticism levelled against it of the lack of conformity to an overall scheme, says: "From the romantic aspect of visual beauty Bath is incomparably more lovely than its theoretically more perfect rivals, and in the same way the unorthodoxy of its individual buildings gives them a liveliness and interest lacking in the more correct designs".[3]

The architect John Wood was responsible for the first phase of town planning in Bath. Settling in the city in 1727, he was soon engaged in the laying out of the area from Queen Square to King's Circus. Together with his son who became, after his father's death in 1754, the chief architect in the town, John Wood inspired half a century of continuous development. During this time the more enclosed atmosphere, created by the first period of building, gave way to the sweeping lines and open vistas of the Royal Crescent, the Lansdown district and the streets and squares on the flank of the hill-side between them. After the Bath Improvement Act of 1789, much of the central area of the city was remodelled, partly on the ancient street-lines, while in the last decades of the century the Bathwick "new town" marked the high-water of geometric planning. Bath thus shows four phases of its Classical townscape in four fairly well-defined districts—the altered and comparatively irregular central area; the finely proportioned squares and terraces of John Wood the Elder; the more open and curvaceous building in the north-west of the town by the younger Wood and his contemporaries; and the altogether more massive and uncompromisingly regular forms dominated by Great Pulteney Street (fig. 61).

The first of these regions contains a type of townscape found to some extent in almost all the older urban areas of Britain. This is the "altered-medieval" form, with Renaissance styling, that is so characteristic of the older streets referred to in the last chapter, in such places as York and Warwick, Hereford and Norwich, Winchester, Durham, Chester and Newbury, and in parts of dozens of small towns and large cities scattered throughout the country. In Bath the central area has a fully metamorphosed character, and, unlike many other altered city cores, only retains the general road pattern, together with some irregularity of building-plan

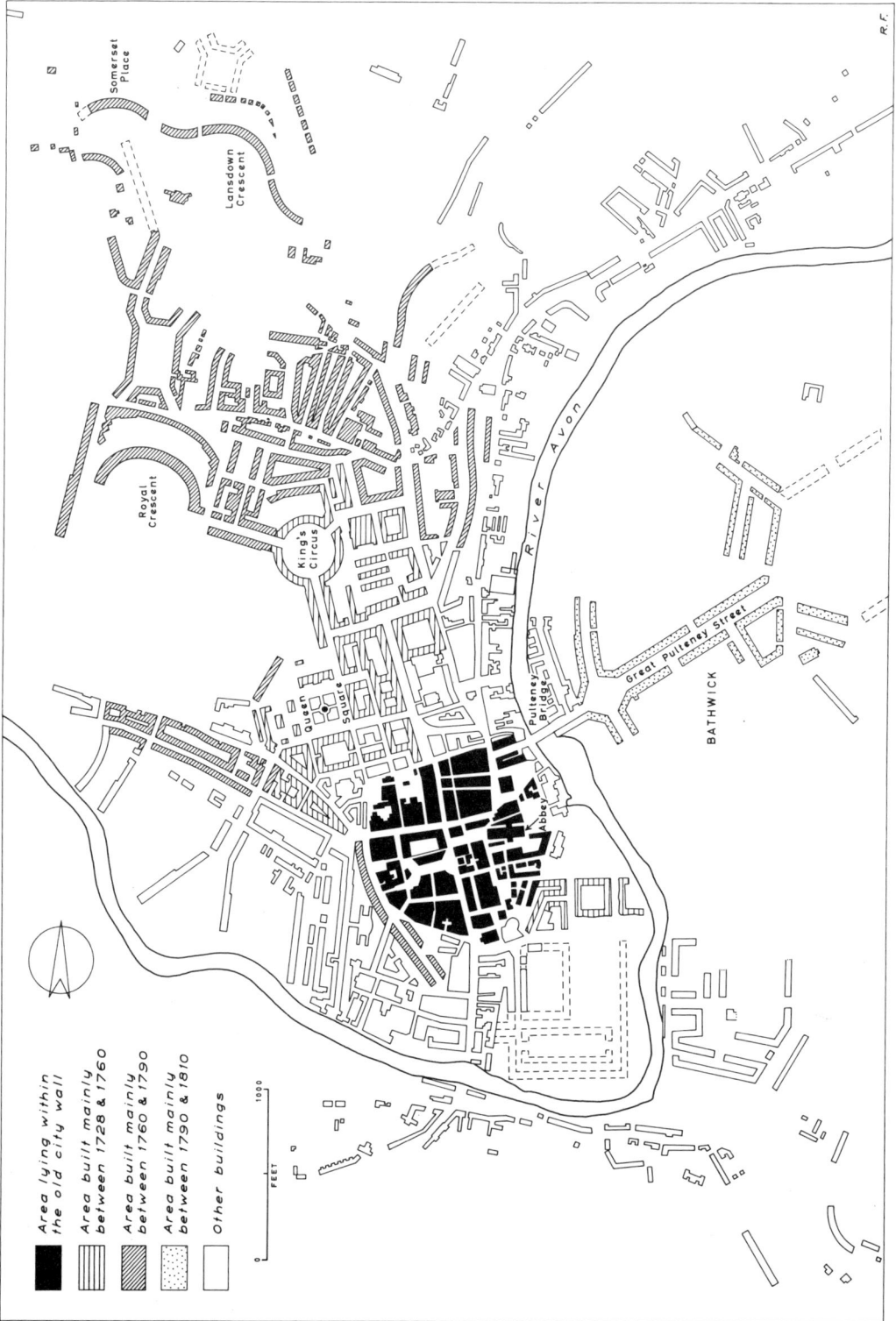

Fig. 60. The buildings of Bath (after Ison)

Legend:
- Area lying within the old city wall
- Area built mainly between 1728 & 1760
- Area built mainly between 1760 & 1790
- Area built mainly between 1790 & 1810
- Other buildings

FEET
0   1000

Somerset Place
Lansdown Crescent
Royal Crescent
King's Circus
Queen Square
River Avon
Pulteney Bridge
Abbey
Great Pulteney Street
BATHWICK

R.F.

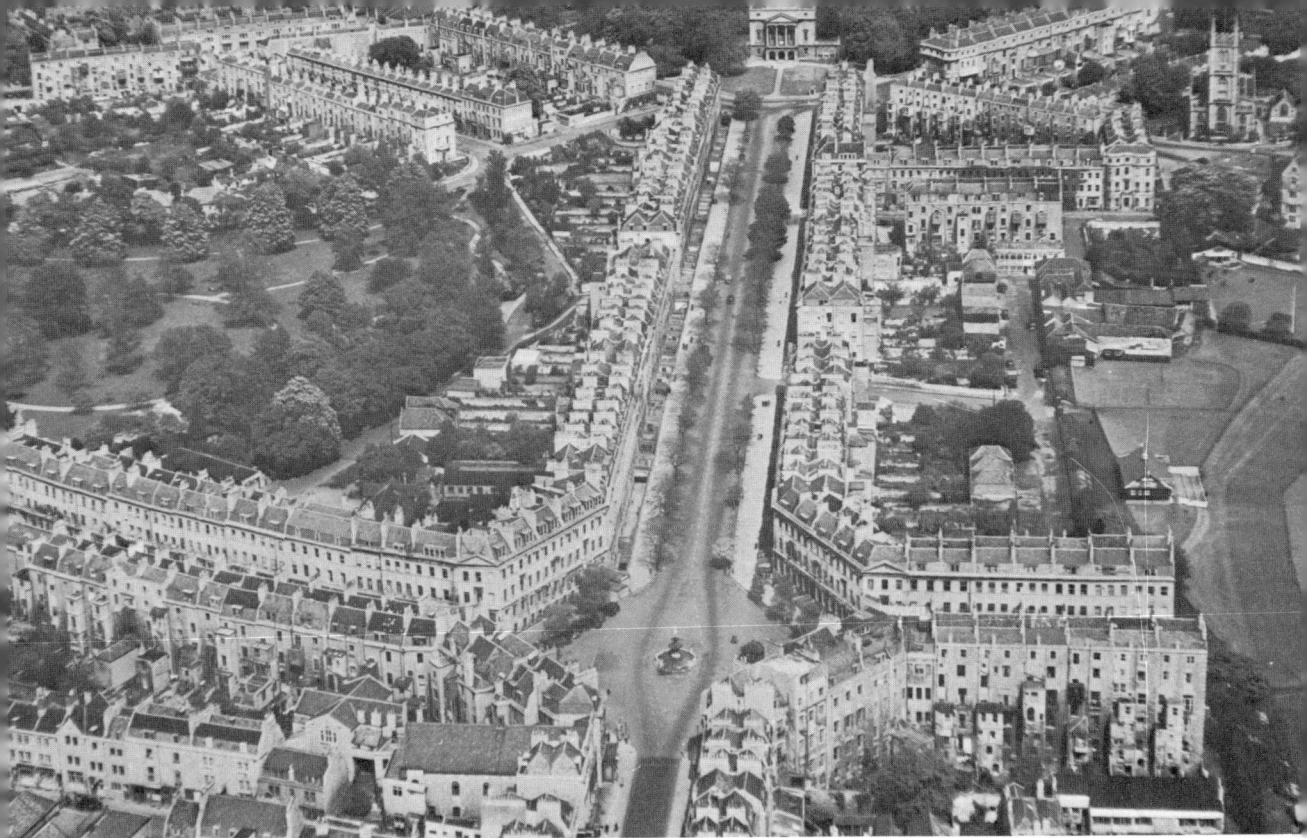

Fig. 61. Bathwick, with Great Pulteney Street

Fig. 62. Bath crescents, including Lansdown Crescent

Fig. 63. A corner house
in Bath

and roof-line, to suggest the outlines of the medieval settlement. The design of the blocks of buildings, on each face, is largely Georgian, and although they form the modern shopping and business centre, they are well preserved and little spoiled above first-floor level. In some of the narrowest streets and precincts the added attraction of the occasional bow window, or some decorative moulding of Victorian vintage, spices the composition, but gable ends, high-pitched roofs and Gothic windows are conspicuously absent.

The second of Bath's town-patterns is best represented by Queen Square and the Circus. These two monuments to the elder Wood are the Bath equivalent of some of the best London squares. They have a metropolitan air, though the golden stonework and the splendid trees provide scenes of greater beauty than do many of the brick-lined vistas of the capital city. To the north and west of the Circus the extensively planned streets and parks make a third definable zone of city-building. This area contains the Royal Crescent and the Lansdown building groups, and includes, as essential ingredients of the architectural landscape, green spaces, arrangements of trees and selectively placed shrubberies. As a piece of town design which consciously tries to adapt itself to the conditions of the local environment, the serpentine forms made by Lansdown Crescent and its neighbouring terrace, Somerset Place (fig. 62), are superb. Here is an attempt to fit the Classical townscape to the green English hill-side. The steep coomb which drops away from this fine group of houses is still in its original form—smoothly curved like the crescent above it—but with a sufficiency of nature's irregularities to give a feeling of liveliness and individuality to each view from the many parlour and bedroom windows. The Royal Crescent, for all its architectural perfections, may seem too formal and majestic for contemporary domestic conditions, but its elevated position, and the spacious turf and trees sweeping away before it, make its contribution to the urban design one of outstanding importance.

Still within the eighteenth-century building-period, but much less typical of the rest of the city, is the unfinished "new town", the completed parts of which lie across the River Avon from Pulteney Bridge. Here, characterised by the 1,500 feet of Great Pulteney Street, is the area known as Bathwick, in which is mirrored, but briefly, the image of the great Baroque cities of Europe (fig. 61). The site of the building here is flat; the streets are mostly quite straight and very wide; and the overall impression is one of extreme monotony and heaviness. It is fortunate that this style of planning was quickly abandoned and that the lighter touch, associated with the early nineteenth century in architecture, soon replaced it in the continued modelling of Bath.

It is generally conceded that the architects of Bath, while importing Renaissance standards and styles, built to a scale appropriate to the English landscape. They rarely made attempts, however, to harmonise with nature, and their neglect of the Avon as a guiding line for the streets, or as a feature to be enhanced by open spaces and promenades, marks their planning as thoroughly formal and un-Romantic: and Classicism can become ridiculous when it is nothing more than a mask, as it is in the corner house illustrated in fig. 63. But while parts of Bath lack the intimate shapes and the gentle accommodation of nature which characterise some of the finest building of the late nineteenth century, it makes an excellent setting for mid-twentieth-century building. Such works, for example, as the recent bus centre, composed in simple bold forms, sit quite well in the old surroundings. This ability to absorb contemporary styles, combined with the wearing qualities of Bath stone—so that even the rear quarters of the big blocks have a mellow aspect— enables Bath to go on growing as one of Britain's most beautiful cities.

Many examples of the Classical townscape of the seventeenth and eighteenth centuries survive in parts of central London. John Summerson, introducing *Georgian London*,[4] identifies three main phases of the building of the capital between the years 1600 and 1800. From the two ancient nuclei of the Cities of London and Westminster (together with the line of palaces "like Oxford Colleges" along the Strand) the main accretions in the two-hundred-year period were, firstly, the irregular development of housing, business premises and private estates or palaces around the fringe of the medieval city; secondly, the "regular development in small units chiefly of the late seventeenth and early eighteenth centuries", includ- ing the houses and squares around Covent Garden, St. James's and north of Picca- dilly; and thirdly, the "regular development in large units" of the early Georgian period, starting with Hanover Square and working north and west beyond Oxford Street, and as far as Hyde Park (fig. 64). Although the outlines and masses of the townscapes in these three phases are broadly similar to those of eighteenth-century Bath, important contrasts can be observed. In the capital city a very large part of the domestic building was in brick—red in the seventeenth century, changing gradually to yellow and grey in the eighteenth. Again, though the early period of the Classical town is, in London, a much longer one than in Bath, there is, for its size, much less variety in the street-plan than is the case in the West Country spa. Terrace after terrace, and square after square, on predominantly flat and unin- teresting sites, add up to an inflexible gridiron system unrelieved by changing contours.

A very large proportion of the buildings that lined the streets of old London has disappeared, but the basic plan of the streets in the West End is largely unchanged to-day from what it was two hundred years ago. Some good examples of almost un- spoilt Georgian London exist in Bloomsbury. To judge from the survivals here, the length and width of the streets and the spaciousness of the squares made most of the buildings of the early Classical period look comparatively modest, while the well- disciplined frontages of the houses made a scene of refinement and yet of domes- ticity. Bedford Square and parts of Gower Street still survive in unmarred beauty. It was not until the London of John Nash and Thomas Cubitt that, with a change from brick to stucco, from entirely straight lines to a mixture of straights and curves, and from modest to monumental scale, the most confident of the Classical lines were drawn in the metropolis (see Chapter 6). The legacy of the first phase of Classical townscape in London is best appreciated from the aerial view of part of the West End, which shows the extensive road system of rectilinear form mostly dating from that time (fig. 65).

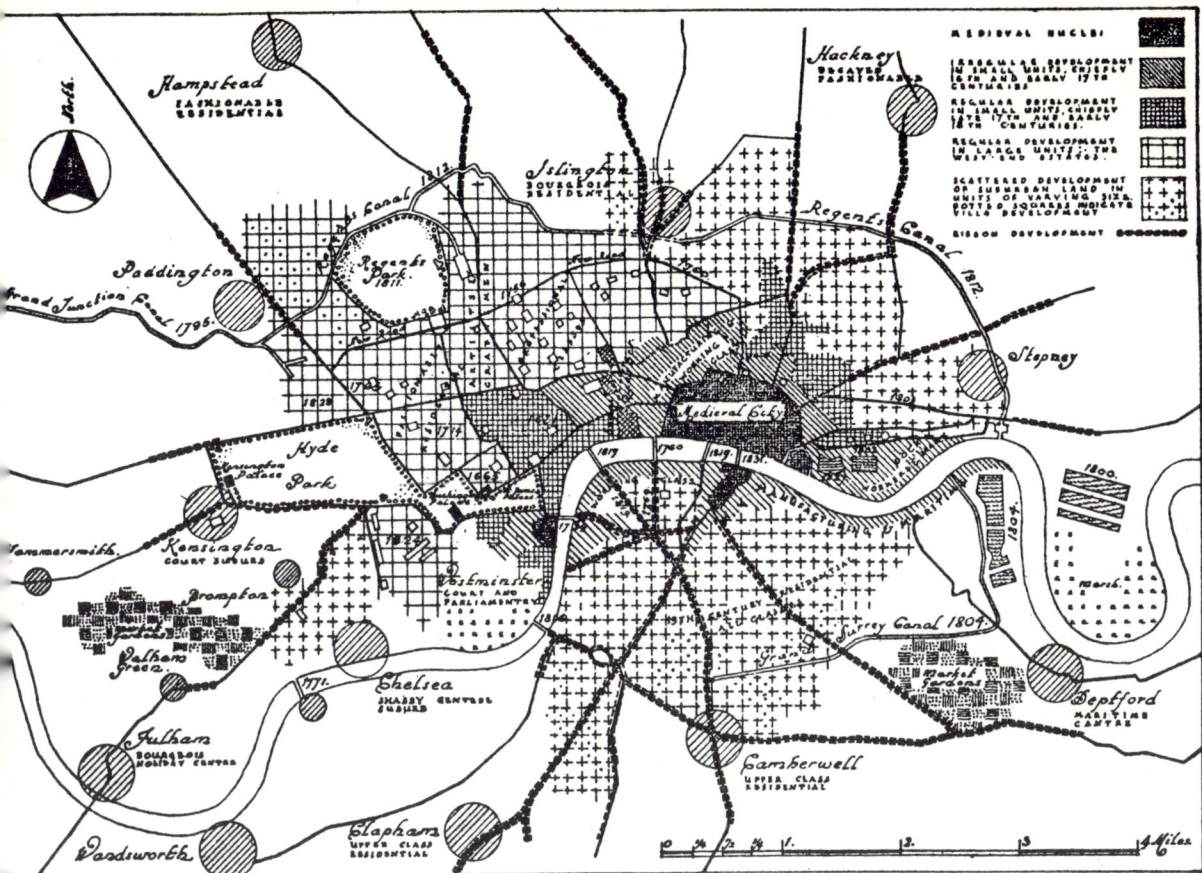

Fig. 64. The development of London up to 1830 (after Summerson)

Fig. 65. Aerial view of part of the West End of London

Fig. 66. Castle Rock and the New Town, Edinburgh

Fig. 67. The principal streets of the original plan of the New Town, Edinburgh

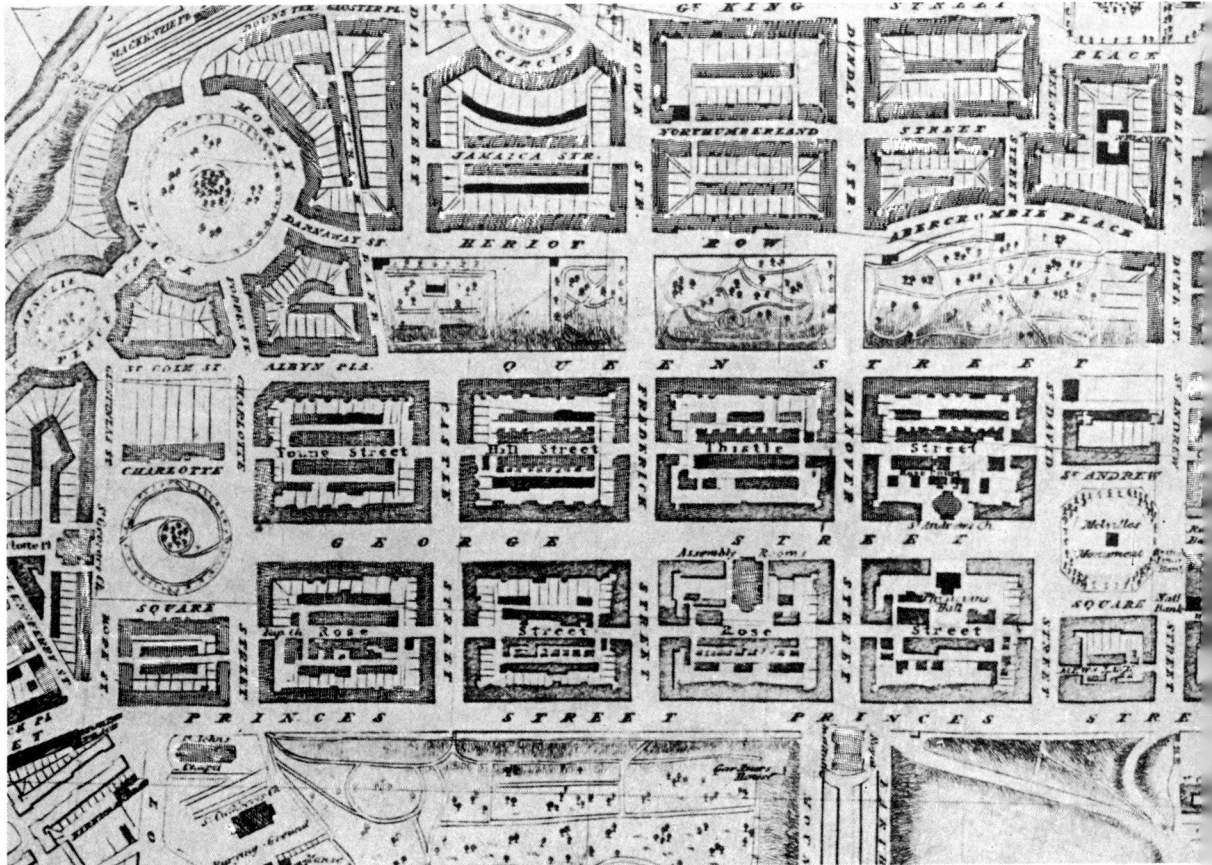

The most natural conclusion to a consideration of the first stage of British Classical town-building is supplied by Edinburgh's New Town. This mainly eighteenth-century scheme, together with its subsequent development, is the most outstanding example, apart from that of Bath, of the architectural planning of an extensive town area anywhere, and at any time, in Britain. The boldness and clarity of the New Town, combined with the contrasting magnificence of the Old Town on its mysterious, craggy hill, give Edinburgh the richest town landscape in these islands. The Classical building to the north of Castle Rock spans more than half a century of activity, but the initial scheme for the layout of a formal street pattern was drawn up by James Craig, who laid the foundation stone of the first house in the area in 1767. As in the Bath of John Wood the Elder, the first streets and squares in Edinburgh's New Town are rigidly rectilinear, while work that followed later takes on a greater freedom of line, and introduces a range of curves in the many crescents and circuses. But in the Scottish town, the first phase is much more extensive than it is in Bath, and is in no way affected by nearness to an ancient nucleus where complex street patterns and building-lines press to the borders of the formal work of the mid-eighteenth-century planners. This first stage of development in Edinburgh continued to dominate the lines of future building in the northern part of the city throughout the nineteenth century, and by its strategic position, overlooked, and yet not overpowered by, the Castle, it plays a role of the utmost importance in the design of the Scottish capital (fig. 66).

Craig's plan is dramatically simple, and the additions to it are rarely complex. The original scheme was based on George Street, which runs along a crest, and is paralleled by Princes Street on the south and Queen Street on the north. Two fine squares—St. Andrew Square and Charlotte Square—mark the termination of the original layout to east and west (fig. 67). With the exception of Princes Street and the area to the south and west of St. Andrew Square, where practically no Georgian frontages exist to-day, a large part of the rest of the individual structures of the first part of the New Town are in their original form which was, though subject to a general regularity, not one of rigid uniformity.[5]

No words can give a fair impression of the buildings which have come to occupy these streets and squares. The New Town is, to some extent, a Scottish version of Bath. Its tough, tall buildings, made of magnificent sandstones from the nearby quarries of Craigleith, together with other fine local building-stones, are recognisable immediately for their stylish adherence to the prevailing mode of architectural design, especially in the building which is wholly or in part by a native of Scotland —Robert Adam. There is, however, a weightier impression made by almost every line and shape in the northern city. "Sets" of hard granite blocks make up the wide cobbled roads; massive lintels, steps and curb-stones form strongly horizontal lines giving support to the general pattern; detail on façades of buildings is, on the whole, suppressed. The weightiness is present, too, in the chunky iron railings in the fronts of houses and around the grass-plots in the squares, while the back premises of the main terraces have a mountainous quality in keeping with the heights of neighbouring Castle Rock. On a smaller scale are to be found in the small service streets and mews behind the main thoroughfares (for example, Rose Street and Thistle Street) fine stone houses and cottages. These streets are now almost totally unsuited

Fig. 68. Part of the Royal Circus, Edinburgh

to the functions they are serving and contain sections that are virtually slums, and yet there is an undying dignity even in the most depressed of these quarters, largely owing to an unerring sense of proportion, combined with a near-perfect building material.

74

The Craig plan was not, as has been said, carried out in uniform and symmetrical building groups of, for example, the type found in Bathwick, and a purist might point out that, on its own, the area between Princes Street and Queen Street would not be enough to justify the international reputation of Edinburgh's Classical buildings. This would be true, but the standards set by the first architects were maintained, and in some cases raised, by their followers in the New Town area—for instance, in the scheme of building lying to the north of Queen Street, and in the series of impressive circuses which include the Royal Circus (fig. 68) and Moray Place—and so it is partly as a pointer to the way things would go that the early New Town is so important. There is, moreover, something very pleasing about slight irregularities contained within the lines of an expansive plan (fig. 69), and Craig's rectangular blocks might well have acquired a somewhat ruthless character if they had all been designed to a similar pattern.

Edinburgh's early Classical townscape has a regional as well as a period quality. Whereas English building in towns of the same period has noticeably horizontal lines, and rarely seems concerned with impressiveness and bulk, there is a grandness of scale in the Scottish building which comes later in town planning developments south of the border. There was not a conscious setting of fashion in the north, but there was continuity of a tradition which in the case of Edinburgh may well have been encouraged by the characteristically towering medieval buildings which grew up, owing to lack of space, in the walled Old Town. Nevertheless, in New Town, Edinburgh, there is preserved an urban region in which the sense of proportion in streets, open sites and buildings is of a most sensitive kind, and where the utmost consideration of the arrangement of space (so often lavished elsewhere in Britain on individual houses) has been given to a whole series of town-building projects which are as splendid now as when they were carried out well over a century ago (fig. 70).

Fig. 69. Houses in Queen Street, Edinburgh

Fig. 70. Crescent, squares and terraces of Edinburgh New Town

6. *The Renaissance in British Townscape*
continued

ALTHOUGH major town-building projects occurred in a few large towns and cities during the eighteenth century, in other urban areas the period was one of alteration rather than of fundamental replanning or redesigning. However, towards the end of the century, in addition to the great industrial growths to be described in the next chapter, many smaller towns emerged from their village beginnings, and, in particular, many spas and resorts appeared, which followed the lead of Bath. In tiny seaside places as remote as Aberayron on Cardigan Bay, and in the great resorts of Brighton and Cheltenham, in Sidmouth in Devon and in Scarborough in the North Riding of Yorkshire, there appeared a new type of townscape. Although architects had already produced a wide range of variations on Renaissance themes, well illustrated in the contrasting works of William Chambers and the brothers Adam, and not all Georgian building was as severely plain as the earliest terraces of Bath or the squares of Bloomsbury, nevertheless the comprehensively planned areas of towns before the year 1800 were architecturally chaste and almost unadorned. But now there appeared, with the first decades of the nineteenth century, an increasing tendency towards the abandonment of pure Renaissance formulae. The decoration of façades of buildings, the use of wrought-ironwork, rich cornices, canopies, shutters, bow windows, rounded bays and even sculpture, produced an entirely new prospect in the urban scene. Yet all this innovation—for so it must have seemed at the time—was still contained within a Classical mould, and respected the broad principle of putting proportion and regularity before all other considerations in building-construction. There was an increasing willingness, however, to break away from absolute symmetry; building-lines were staggered, and the heights of roofs were more varied. As more and more landowners sought to improve and develop their estates in the neighbourhood of the growing towns, and as more and more architects appeared, to meet the growing demand for their services, the results were a greater diversity in the morphology of the town, and a new vitality and peculiar charm ensued which is especially English—a happy blend of the disciplined and the humane. Towns that were built at this time retain an air of spacious ease, and foster the appreciation of good living. Their good qualities are traceable as much to their layouts and design as to their original functions—functions which were not always connected with the leisurely pursuits of the aristocracy. There was considerable commercial and residential building in industrial areas, ports and county towns, much of it now in decay or entirely replaced. Though perhaps less elegant than that of the principal holiday and pleasure towns, this building was well planned and of singular attractiveness.

Fig. 71. Aberayron, Cardiganshire

An interesting example of a planned town of the early nineteenth century is Aberayron, a small place of 1,160 inhabitants on the shores of Cardigan Bay. It is almost the same size as Lavenham,[1] though it covers a wider area and possesses a distinctly more urban air. The contrast between Aberayron and the Suffolk town could not in fact be more complete; in shape of buildings, street-plan and architectural detail the two towns are poles apart. Yet both owe their existence to a period of industry and trade. The town at the mouth of the little Aeron river is a most unexpected sight in its west coast setting. It has a rectilinear plan, with well-spaced dwellings, warehouses and hotels, and a large public green and spacious harbour-walks (fig. 71). The houses are mostly modest in size and style and of a simpler appearance than the more fashionable buildings of similar date in the wealthier and less windswept residential towns of distant England. However, the placing of larger buildings in the centres and at the ends of terraces, to avoid monotony; the characteristic rusticated quoins and the mildly decorative lintels; and the whole feeling of neatness and good taste, make this little Welsh seaside town a model instance of the second phase of British Classical townscape.

Fig. 72. The Royal Pavilion, Brighton

Although the building of Aberayron has been linked with the name of John Nash, no authentic record of its architectural planning seems to have been discovered. The town itself, which is of entirely nineteenth-century origin, was the inspiration of the Rev. Alban Thomas Jones Gwynne, who was responsible for the development of a harbour and shipbuilding yards on his estate, and must have taken a large part in the decision to plan the rest of the town, in consultation with architects and builders.[2] Undoubtedly one mind sponsored the harmonious building groups throughout the town. Gwynne's enterprise was a calculated piece of economic planning, aimed at the establishment of a port for the transhipment of goods from coastal vessels to a wide agricultural hinterland. For the first half of the nineteenth century the town flourished, and not only attracted much trade by the sea routes, but also developed a number of industries connected with shipbuilding. From fifty to seventy ships were built at Aberayron in a period of about forty years, until steamships and the railway ended the boom. The town has never had cause for expansion since then, but there has been just sufficient demand for its attractions as a holiday place to prevent a decline. There is thus preserved a small Welsh Classical town in almost exactly its original form.

Unlike Aberayron, Brighton is not homogeneous: its Classical quarters were added to a settlement of about 3,000 inhabitants towards the end of the eighteenth century, and have since become surrounded by successive, and increasingly extensive, phases of building. The development which took place roughly between 1790 and 1830, however, is the most distinctive part of the present urban scene. In contrast to Aberayron, Brighton was essentially a spa, and one enjoying royal patronage. As E. W. Gilbert says, "Fame as a health resort and the building of the Royal Pavilion as a seaside residence for the Prince of Wales, afterwards George IV, were the main causes of Brighton's extraordinary expansion".[3] It is not surprising, therefore, that here are some of the grandest examples of late Georgian building. Although nothing else in Britain, much less in Brighton, can be compared with it, and in architectural terms it is unclassifiable in spite of its orientalism, the Royal Pavilion sets the key for the whole orchestration of the town: to pursue the musical analogy, the Pavilion is the solo instrument, or the prima donna, in a composition backed by a fine but lesser accompaniment. Completed by John Nash in 1820, the present elaborate structure is an audacious yet sensitive remodelling of an earlier building (fig. 72). The Pavilion expressed perfectly, if in extreme form, the vogue for subtle curves, broken skylines and delicate tracery, all built up on an orderly Classical foundation. It is in the planned districts of Kemp Town and Brunswick Town, both of the 1820's, and other layouts, in terrace and crescent, that the flowing style of the period is found applied to the townscape itself, while down through the Steine later alterations have not destroyed the fine lines of the earlier building. Even without its Pavilion, Brighton is rich, with its bow fronts and bay windows, its canopies and verandas. It is built for pleasurable—meaning sociable—living. The finest houses overlook the public thoroughfare, and can in turn be overlooked by the frank and admiring public gaze. The house-block and the street form one feature, as they did in medieval times, but they are now expressly designed to be a place of common architectural value.

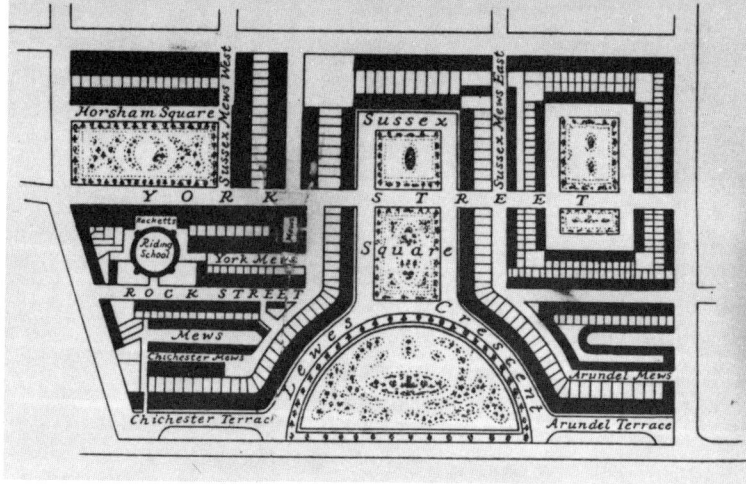

Fig. 73. The Kemp Town
Estate of 1825

Fig. 74. Kemp Town
in 1930

The area known as Kemp Town was built on an open piece of downland over-looking the sea, to the east of the old town of Brighthelmston. To-day it is an excellent example of how the "Regency" scene has survived in the town landscape. A comparison between the map (fig. 73) and the air photograph (fig. 74) makes possible an examination of present-day Kemp Town against the background of the original ground-plan of the streets and houses. In the plan of the estate (of 1825) the severest symmetry has been avoided in the alignment of the terraces and open spaces on either side of Sussex Square, and this characteristic, together with the rounded corners of the two wings of Lewes Crescent, are features which are in keeping with the general tendency of the period to avoid repetitive "chess-board" systems with their sharp, right-angled, criss-cross streets. Even so, the blue print for Kemp Town has something of the "children's building-brick" look about it—in common with the much smaller estates of suburban development of present times—and the layout of paths and plants in the gardens repeats this rather petty formality. But the view of Kemp Town to-day, from the air at least, is dominated as much by the irregular form of the green spaces as it is by the bold lines of the architectural plan, and the curves of the terraces are seen to branch out into the thin, winding foot-paths in the half-circle of gardens which faces the promenade.

Fig. 75. Buildings in Kemp Town, Brighton

Illustrated so well in the example of Kemp Town, the late Georgian townscape, when well preserved, has probably never looked better than it does to-day. Its individual buildings take kindly to minor alterations if these are sympathetically handled and, in some of its boldest designs, this period of building has the timeless quality that makes it as right for our own age as it was for the age from which it dates (fig. 75).

Of all the pleasure-towns of the early nineteenth century, none survives more completely than Cheltenham. No major change in its function, even in the mid-twentieth century, has come to disturb the late Georgian and early Victorian scenes of this spa and holiday resort at the foot of the Cotswold Hills. Called a "Regency Town" for want of a better definition, Cheltenham saw its main period of growth (up to the First World War) in the decades from 1810 to 1850. In 1806 an early map shows that the town consisted of nothing more than a long street with a few shorter ones running at right-angles to it.[4] As a health resort already attracting visitors from London, it probably had, even at this early date, the beginnings of a feeling of urbanity, for many of the house fronts in the High Street had been re-shaped in the Georgian mode, and the side streets were made of bold new terraces in the fashionable style. Nevertheless, John Goding, describing Cheltenham at the opening of the nineteenth century, says, "Emerging from obscurity, it yet retained all the characteristics of a rural village".[5]

Progress in town-building in Cheltenham was accelerated after the Napoleonic Wars. The estate of Montpellier was being laid out by the time of Samuel Bettinson's "Plan of the Town of Cheltenham" in 1825. The Lansdown estate followed soon afterwards, and the Pittville estate was nearly complete in 1853.[6] Several sources of the Cheltenham waters were discovered at widely-spaced sites, a fact which aided the architects in their preference for spacious planning. Although there is little demand for these waters to-day, their original location was a factor of some importance in determining the form of the early town plan:[7] so, too, were the shapes of the High Street and of the old road from Evesham which crossed it at right-angles. The very interesting web of roads which has evolved, although made up for the most part of straight lines, nevertheless follows the changing directions of the original thoroughfares. The resulting street-plan is more like a loosely-hung net than a rigid gridiron (fig. 76): the bold avenues are never too long, and never assume the hard, impersonal lines of ceremonial streets. Confirming this tendency to avoid highly formal arrangements of streets and buildings is the offsetting of the Queen's Hotel at the end of the Promenade, so that its axis is well to one side of the centre of the road. Some of the conditions of its original site and function have made Cheltenham a spread-out, spacious town, but it is to the credit of its early developers and architects that the town's initial advantages have been used to the full.

The town plan of Cheltenham consists of developments on either side of the long, gently-meandering High Street—the original main street of the settlement, when it was nothing more than a small ribbon of houses on the London to Gloucester road. The spacious, formal estates standing well back from the High Street have a self-contained quality arising in large measure from ground plans of crescent, circus and square. There is no real town centre, probably because the "gracious living" of the times for which this town was planned did not require a market square or a centre-piece of municipal administration. Prizing elegance, calmness, spaciousness and decorum, the town became a sort of highly refined suburbia. The areas of fine private building, with their open spaces, were predecessors of the modern "neighbourhoods", but with all the emphasis on appearances, either from the "first-floor front", or from the street beneath. Cheltenham is perhaps the most perfect example of its type of town. The Promenade is a thoroughfare of international distinction, and everywhere a stylish and delicate architecture flowers.

With foresight and a sense of social responsibility that we could well emulate to-day, the early builders of Cheltenham planted the streets, avenues and parks with trees. Now, one in every ten acres of the town is public park; when wide, tree-lined pavements and precincts with gardens and shrubberies are added to this area, they make a total green network of exceptional scale and beauty. The official town guidebook states that forty miles of streets have mature avenues of forty thousand trees. There is no lovelier town scenery in Britain than the white and cream painted stucco buildings of Cheltenham as they appear through a filigree of branches and leaves (figs. 77 and 78).

Fig. 76. The street plan of Cheltenham (O.S. 6″ to mile, 1954)

Before becoming lost in architectural reverence, however, we must recognise the two chief weaknesses of the "Regency" townscape in Cheltenham. These are first, the areas of poorer dwellings built originally for the classes of people who serviced the town, and second, the totally undesigned back premises of the main building-blocks which are as important to the whole urban scene as are the parts facing the

Fig. 77. Buildings overlooking The Promenade, Cheltenham

Fig. 78. The Promenade, Cheltenham

Fig. 79. A side street in Cheltenham

main streets. An example of the former is seen in fig. 79. This street, long committed to the penalty of death by neglect, plays no part in the planned scenery which comes near to it on almost all sides. The houses in the terrace have only a lick of stucco, and doorways with half-round fanlights, to distinguish them from the most uninspired kind of back street dwellings of industrial Britain. The second weakness is dramatically evident in the decaying Lansdown Crescent. Now near to ruin, this ambitious design, which was unfortunately planned with its front facing north, and convex, still retains some dignity, in spite of the scars of age and the ravages caused by modern plumbing and television masts: but, together with the rear of Lansdown Place, across the way, the back premises of the crescent make a landscape of un-relieved hideousness (fig. 80). Throughout Cheltenham, similar scenes occur, in-variably in brick, since the bulk of the building in the town is only fronted with stucco, or occasionally with stone. Few industrial cities have worse examples, on a small scale, of the tyranny of uncontrolled and undesigned brickwork.

In spite of these limitations, Cheltenham is a gay-looking town—even, on a sunny day, a dashing one. The street-furniture has been designed as if it was meant as a valuable part of urban life. The benches are roomy and rather grand, and are intended for rest and not just for casual perching, and the old tramway stanchions are quite elegantly adapted to the needs of modern street lighting. In places, owing to the wide streets, there is less traffic confusion than in many towns and the pedes-trian seems to be accorded some respect as if in memory of the lost days referred to by John Goding. "The far-famed 'musical promenades' were held here (Mont-pellier Walk) during the autumn months, and with the illuminations, the rows of gas lamps on each side, and the gay throng of promenaders, presented a scene of such attraction, such as has never since been witnessed in Cheltenham."[8]

"Royal" Leamington Spa is, in its central areas, a similar type of town to Cheltenham, and falls into the late Classical period of townscape. Many blocks of buildings from the Warwickshire town could be exchanged for similar groups in Cheltenham, and neither their design nor the materials of their construction would

86

Fig. 80. The rear of Lansdown Crescent, Cheltenham

cause surprise. But the adaptation of the site on the banks of the Leam to make a Midland resort has resulted in a less well-integrated architectural plan than did the town-building on either side of the Cheltenham High Street. When, in the year 1810, a plan for a "New Town" at Leamington Priors was drawn up, the site chosen was not in the immediate neighbourhood of the early village of Leamington, but on the rising ground to the north of it. Here, beyond the limits of the flood-waters of the river, the highly-regimented plots of building land were marked out (fig. 81). The poorly-drained land along the Leam was later improved as an open space, thus making permanent the separation of the early village-nucleus from the major piece of town-planning. The layout of roads to-day, immediately to the north and south of the main bridging point of the river, reveals how this early phase of Leamington's history has controlled subsequent development (fig. 82).

Fig. 81. A plan of Leamington in 1843

Fig. 82. Leamington today

Classical Leamington thus starts rather abruptly, where The Parade meets the Jephson and the Pump Room Gardens. At this point, the main street has an unfinished look as if it had originally been intended as an approach to larger and more expansive building groups in the neighbourhood of the somewhat inconsequential Pump Room. The chess-board pattern of streets on either side of The Parade is unimaginative, and the fine buildings in the major terraces mask a succession of back streets consisting of depressing service-buildings and semi-slums (fig. 83). On the other hand, there are some splendid examples of the genius for street scenery which is characteristic of the period. For instance, the upper part of The Parade, where a levelling-out of the land gives the street a more enclosed feeling than it has in its sloping section, has a feeling of composure and refinement, and the attractive ground-floor shop-fronts, the splendid wrought-ironwork of the balconies above and the lines of well-shaped windows set in the gleaming stucco, make a delightful composition (fig. 84). Again, Lansdown Crescent is a piece of fine design, and has in addition the attractions of well-placed trees and shrubberies (fig. 85). But it might well be argued that it is the Jephson Gardens, with their Romantic layout of paths and flower-beds, and their consciously irregular placing of trees to create a "naturalistic" setting for the winding River Leam, that gives Leamington its special flavour, while the later Victorian villas in Newbold Terrace and Kenilworth Road are also an essential part of the character of the whole spa. Since consideration of these examples would involve another period of townscape, their characteristics must be described in a later chapter.

Fig. 83. A back street, Leamington

Fig. 84. Shops in the upper Parade, Leamington

Fig. 85. Lansdown Crescent, Leamington

The name of John Nash has already been mentioned in this chapter: it is inseparable from much provincial town-building of the early eighteen-hundreds. Furthermore, the metropolitan work of this great architect and town planner crowns the late period of Classical townscape. Nash's schemes for linking the high-class residential areas of the West End estates with Westminster, by means of spacious roads, squares and parks, and his plan to extend the residential area itself, in landscaped surroundings, beyond the New Road (as Marylebone Road was then called), are well known. The effect that this work had on the contemporary London scene is described in such vivid terms by John Summerson[9] that a further account of this subject here would be at best mere reiteration; but a brief reference to the place of this phase of building in the present London setting is essential. The map (fig. 86) shows the extent of the area which Nash was responsible for completing between 1811 and 1835. In plan the Nash buildings, in association with their care-fully-contrived open spaces in and around Regent's Park and St. James's Park, make up two major areas of loosely-woven town-fabric joined together by a slack thread of streets. This represents a part only of the projected plans of the great architect, and significant parts of what he did complete have since vanished. Enough remains, however, for a town planner of such noted resolution and foresight as Colin Buchanan to say that "we should be seeking not merely to conserve but to enhance . . ." this heritage.[10] Whatever the future holds for this famous "progression" of buildings across central London, it is a model of what can be done to re-make a part of the vitals of a great city, and for all its occasional grandeur, it is an example of Englishness in its scale and in its tolerance of variety. The variety was, as far as John Nash was concerned, partly a concession, for, in spite of patronage no lower than that of the Crown itself, he often experienced difficulty in pushing his schemes through, and frequently had to allow developers of individual sites to indulge their private whims. But Nash was no formal "geometrician" of architecture, and in his own buildings he has left us everything from Gothic to Baroque to prove his inventiveness and love of the varied and the unexpected.

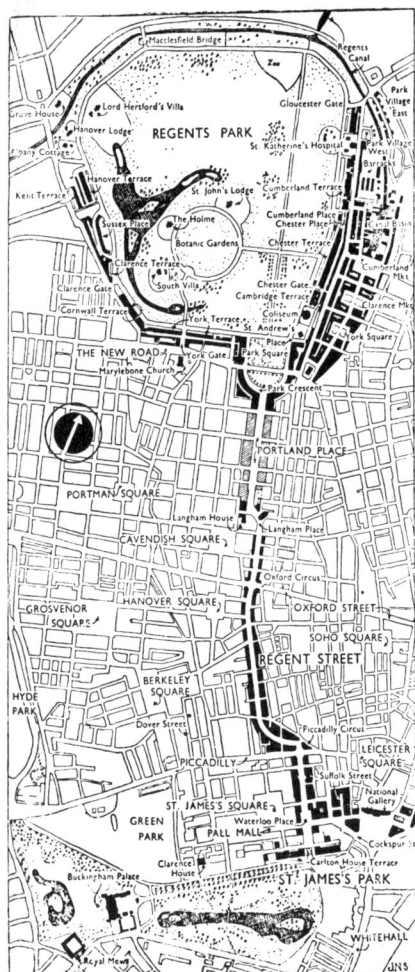

Fig. 86.
The streets,
squares
and parks
laid out
by John Nash,
1811–35

Fig. 87
Part of
Eaton
Square,
Belgravia

Surviving to-day, in the face of restless cross-currents of traffic in Piccadilly, Oxford Street and Marylebone Road, the Nash areas of London are perhaps best appreciated by trying to imagine the capital without them—without Regent Street (even in the altered coat which most of it has worn since the early years of this century); without Trafalgar Square, and without Regent's Park and its surroundings. To-day, to follow the Nash plan from St. James's Park or Trafalgar Square, by way of Waterloo Place to Piccadilly Circus, is sufficient to see the nobility of this conception of town design as it befits a capital city. Unfortunately in these regions the original buildings have almost all gone, and farther up the "Royal Mile" (as the route from Carlton House to Regent's Park was called) the whole of Regent Street has been altered. In Portland Place, however, many beautiful former residences survive, and at Park Crescent can be seen the glad sight of restoration which is bringing back to life one of the loveliest pieces of Georgian planning. From the crescent northwards—spreading out around the borders of Regent's Park—is a world of another age: a city within a city. Most of it is being carefully preserved now, but its squares and avenues are overgrown, and vistas of the buildings must be opened up, by careful thinning of trees, if the townscape is to be fully restored for public enjoyment.

90

The rendered surfaces which covered the buildings of John Nash give the most delightful relief from the grey, yellow or red bricks and the imported building-stones of other parts of London, and they have inspired one of Summerson's most memorable descriptions in the title "the stucco sceptre of the metropolis of George IV".[11] The same surface material was extensively used by Thomas Cubitt who, in association with several architects, built parts of Bloomsbury, and the major part of Belgravia and Pimlico in the late-flowering years of Classical townscape. "Stuccoed London" was thus continued, in patches, around the periphery of the early estates, and the fashion for covering brick was to continue, well into Victorian times, in the extensive terrace-development of such areas as the neighbourhood of Ladbroke Grove which were, in their time, the new suburbs of the growing metropolis.

But to return to the Belgravia region, here if anywhere in London there is to be found a piece of unified, Classical townscape which, because of the excellence of its construction and preservation, is likely to remain not merely as a lasting record of the past, but also as a constantly useful part of the changing city. Houses in a place like Eaton Square (fig. 87) are, of course, not high compared with some contemporary buildings, but are little different from those three- or four-storied horizontal blocks which are so commonly in use as a foil to a neighbouring tower.

Their lively frontal modelling, and the relationship between them and the attractive open spaces, is a brilliant lesson in designing for urban life. The detail of the façades on the north-western side of the square (as seen in the photograph) is a particularly fine instance of the skill of English architects of the early nineteenth century in adapting Classical "bits and pieces" to serve an original composition, in which the overriding consideration of the relationship of the height to the length of the building-blocks is supported by bold horizontal or vertical sequences of columns, pediments, cornices and balustrades. These last do not, however, at any time destroy the unity of the whole shape. The columns in front of the ground-floors "grow" into the balustrade and into the lines of upper-storey windows above them; the row of pediments over the first-floor windows form one long fretted line of gentle angles, which is a subtle echo of the general horizontality. Higher up, the buildings are girdled by a rich cornice with a motif of deeply swung garlands which counter, by their rather voluptuous curves, the tendency to sharpness in the pediments below. Other variations exist, like the projecting sections of the façade at the ends or centres of blocks, which again succeed in enriching without overburdening the total composition. In all, the architecture of Eaton Square is refined, yet bold; formal, yet a little daring; calm, yet alert. No one part of it may be regarded as comparable with the greatest individual masterpieces of its period, but taken as a whole, and in conjunction with the mature gardens which complete its glory, the square is hard to equal as an example of urban design.

The buildings and parks of John Nash, Thomas Cubitt and others of their time are amongst the principal possessions of the capital city. The buildings are fine, not only in their own right but even more because they have been designed to be seen from many angles, and especially from the centre or edges of the parks. They were not, however, planned to be enjoyed from the rear, and, in common with the great blocks of Cheltenham, Leamington and elsewhere, the back premises of Belgravia, for instance, have a totally different character from that of the frontages. Unlike many town areas of this period, especially in the provinces, Belgravia possesses the great advantage of high land values (which, regretfully, is still the principal way in which good architecture comes to be preserved in Britain) and so even the smallest room in a converted stable in the cobbled mews behind Belgrave Square is fashionable, expensive and well maintained. It is interesting to compare illustrations of frontages in Belgrave Square (fig. 88) with the rear quarters of a similar terrace in Belgrave Mews South (fig. 89), and to relate both of these to conditions in Lansdown Crescent, Cheltenham (fig. 80), and behind The Parade at Leamington Spa (fig. 83).

The Classical townscape continues with modifications well beyond the days of George IV and into the Victorian era. Its somewhat chequered progress will be followed in later chapters, but meanwhile it is possible to sum up very briefly the characteristics of the principal periods of this phase of British town-building. The necessarily very few examples which have been used here, and in the previous chapter, to represent a very widespread phase of urban growth could all be called, in the current terminology of art-criticism, "hard-edged": after the medieval towns which, in their most characteristic form, were made from squatting, crooked—even, it may be said, vegetable shapes—the contrast of the town derived from the Renaissance is obvious in its bold, clean lines and ordered layout. From the early days of mid-eighteenth-century Bath, to the period of maximum vitality of the industrial city (see Chapter 7), the Classical period of British townscapes is approximately a century in length. It starts in modest scale and with exactingly-considered proportions, its building groups regarded as small works of architectural completeness, and it ends as a contribution to town planning in at least the architectural sense, though it was to take another century, and a dramatic improvement in working-class conditions, to give to town planning the universal and "missionary" quality that we expect it to have to-day. While society was accepted as a static phenomenon— as it must have seemed to be in the eighteenth century—some splendid solutions were found to the problem of how to build towns to accommodate the material requirements and to satisfy the aesthetic aspirations of those days.

Fig. 88. Part of Belgrave Square

Fig. 89. Belgrave Mews South

7. *New Towns of the Industrial Age*

THE town scenes that have been studied in the last two chapters were products of private enterprise. They demonstrate both the advantages and the disadvantages that accrue to cities from large-scale investment, in land and buildings, by private developers: the advantages are almost all on the side of the wealthier and more "leisured" members of the community; the disadvantages weigh most heavily on the poor. But rich and poor alike, through the closely integrated social structure that once existed, shared the same urban environments, and often the same buildings. The chambermaid employed in one of the great houses in the Royal Crescent at Bath had as much right, if not as much time, to gaze upon the civic glories of that town as had the governess or the head of the household.

It has already been shown that the attention of the Georgian architect was focused on certain parts of his buildings and building groups: he left others—chiefly those which formed the milieu of the servant class—to chance. But since the town at this time was still small, and since large and clearly separated zones of distinctive function had not yet arisen, there was, in architectural terms, much intermingling of the planned and the unplanned, the designed and the undesigned. A private developer and his architect, in the eighteenth and early nineteenth centuries, were subject to no legal control that might have required them to conceive their plans in relationship to those of others operating in the same district. Such harmony as exists in the Georgian cities is due to the influence of a common fashion in building style. Bath itself lacks a general plan, and owes its beauty to a sum of beautiful parts. It is not surprising, therefore, that when living-quarters had to be provided quickly, and on an extensive scale, for workers in new industrial towns, most of these towns suffered from a complete absence of town planning as we understand it (but do not necessarily practise it) to-day. This is not to say that no thought at all was given to design. Indeed, the early industrial towns were in a sense just cheap versions of the Georgian city.

The story of the rise of industrialism in Britain has often been told, but the historical accounts usually lay stress on the technical, economic and social aspects of the expansion, rather than on the appearance of the urban environments in which this expansion was taking place.[1] The national census of 1801 showed that towns like Birmingham, Liverpool, Manchester and Leeds had populations of over

94

50,000, while Sheffield, Rochdale, Newcastle and Nottingham had over 25,000 inhabitants. Although by the end of the nineteenth century all these towns had expanded to many times their former size, they were already, in the early eighteen-hundreds, substantial places, compared, for instance, with many market and sea-side towns in southern England to-day. The first phase of industrial town growth was therefore well under way while the Classical townscape was undergoing the various phases of refinement that were described in Chapters 5 and 6, and the design of the industrial town from the latter part of the eighteenth century to the middle of the nineteenth century reflects, sometimes dimly, sometimes boldly, the notions of taste fostered by the Georgian architects.

The coal, iron and textile industries of central and northern England, South Wales, and the Scottish Lowlands acted as magnets to men in search of increased wages, and especially to those whose jobs were threatened by the Agricultural Revolution of the eighteenth century. The first towns that emerged in the neigh-bourhood of the industrial sites were of diverse types. An extensive nucleus may have existed (Manchester, for example, was a sizeable settlement in the sixteenth century,[2] and Birmingham had a population of about 15,000 at the end of the seventeenth century), but often the nearest small market town gave its name to an area of haphazard development in which open pits, mineshafts, forges or small fac-tories mingled with the farmsteads, meadows and cornfields.

The "town" of the Nottinghamshire coalfield, in the early nineteenth century, is described by the trenchant pen of D. H. Lawrence:

> "Hell Row was a block of thatched, bulging cottages that stood by the brook-side on Greenhill Lane. There lived the colliers who worked in the gin-pits two fields away. The brook ran under the alder trees, scarcely soiled by these little mines, whose coal was drawn to the surface by donkeys that plodded wearily in a circle round the gin. And all over the countryside were these same pits . . . the few colliers and the donkeys burrowing down like ants into the earth, making queer mounds and little black places among the cornfields and the meadows. And the cottages of these coal-miners in blocks and pairs here and there, together with odd farms and homes of the stockingers, straying over the parish, formed the village of Bestwood".[3]

Lawrence's verbal picture is converted into a visual one, and extended over a whole district, by the map of a part of Lancashire between Oldham and Rochdale in 1828 (fig. 90).

It is not easy to assess the extent to which the first of the industrial townscapes survive in our landscape to-day. They are certainly not always recognised for a distinction of building style which in fact they sometimes possess. Much of this type of urban scene has been cleared away, and what is left is high in the priority list in the slum clearance programme. The principal survivals are probably in the mining and textile towns of the uplands in Wales, Lancashire, the West Riding and Scot-land. Here the tough local stone, from which many of the houses were built, made more durable and more attractive homes than did the brick of the Midland Plain;

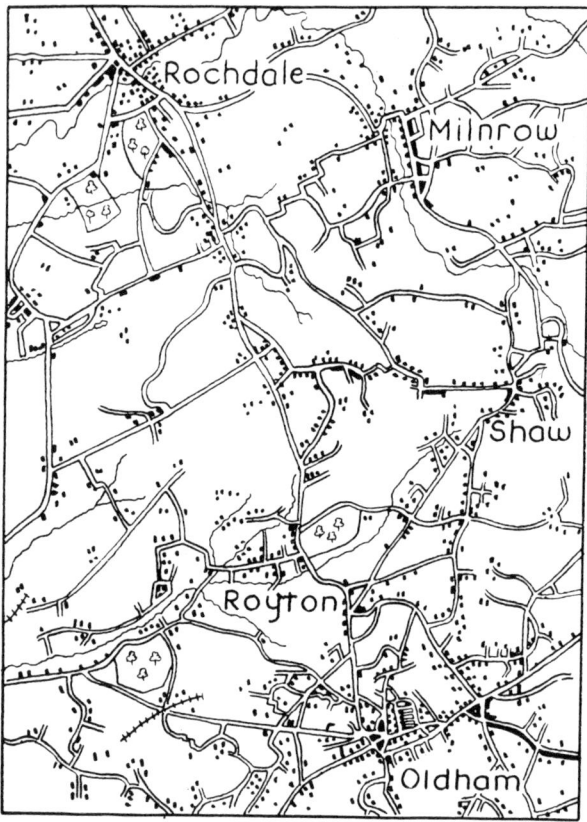

Fig. 90.
The early industrial
landscape in
Lancashire from
Teesdale's map,
1828–9

Fig. 91. A corner of industrial
Lancashire today

and the isolation of some of these settlements from later urban growth has also contributed to their preservation from the periodic process of rebuilding which swept away large parts of many industrial cities. In the small town in the hills, the homes of early industrial workers had much in common with the country cottages from which many of their occupants came, and were, if anything, probably better built and certainly more proof against the risk of fire. In some instances, indeed, quite pleasant little clusters must have resulted from the accidental placing of houses on bits of "waste" land amongst the fields or moorlands (fig. 91). Nevertheless, as we have seen, quite a lot of early industrial towns developed around an older nucleus by the process of adding, piecemeal, small factories and parallel rows of workers' cottages to the old core. Such a town is Bolton, the present form of which in large part dates from the early stages of the Industrial Revolution.

Bolton in 1791 had a population of 11,000,[4] and by 1801 this had risen to 17,146. In the late eighteenth century, therefore, there was already under way a process of urbanisation. "The migration from country cottages to larger premises in the town was gradual and had already begun well before Crompton's time".[5] The sizeable town that existed by 1824 (illustrated by Baines's map of that year, fig. 92) compares well for size with the spas of the period, and, in plan, is neither better nor worse than a great number of much older British towns. The main streets were probably not very different to look at from such places as High Street, Cheltenham

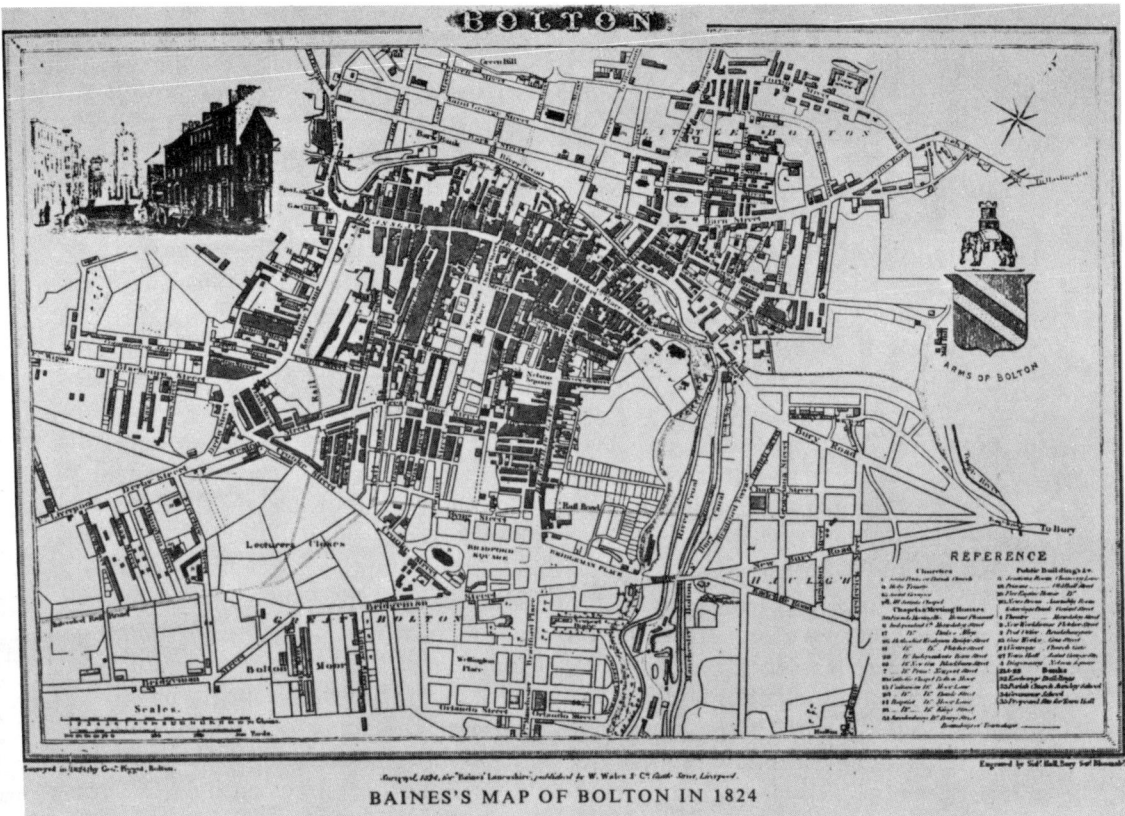

BAINES'S MAP OF BOLTON IN 1824

Fig. 92. Baines's Map of Bolton in 1824

(as the inset to Baines's map shows), and the growing town immediately beyond them had some of the variety and irregularity of the medieval townscape, for example in Church Gate, and some of the studied arrangement of the Renaissance scene, for example around Nelson Square. As can be seen in fig. 93, it was intended to build further terraces, squares and even small crescents to the south of the town, but the coming of the railway, and the demands of industry, frustrated the best of this planning. Between the multitude of small factories scattered about the town, beyond the central area already described, there grew up rows and rows of houses, the worst of them facing each other across narrow courtyards which often ended in the blank workshop wall. But this sort of thing does not give an entirely fair picture of early Bolton, as we shall see.

In the Bolton of to-day industry still comes almost to the heart of the town, and the development plan of the local authority is forced to allow for industrial use all over the map to within yards of the Town Hall itself. The warehouses, chimney-stacks and factory buildings are essential features of the townscape, and most of these are "period pieces"—little altered since the late eighteenth or early nineteenth centuries. Bolton is, in fact, an excellent example of the Georgian industrial town, where the great mills have the proportions and window-arrangements of Classical type (and where a great deal of later building clung to Classical forms, though of a somewhat more decorative kind, as in the case of the splendid Town Hall with its Baroque tower, and of the bright red-brick Italianate railway station). As to the business, commercial and central residential districts of the town, there can still be savoured here much of the character of the eighteenth century. In spite of the new shopping-blocks which, interestingly enough, are being designed to retain the scale and shapes of the Georgian period—even though they are not in any sense historic imitations—there is no difficulty in recognising the predominance of the simple façades of earlier date. The line of almost all the streets in Baines's map is still there, and, apart from the Victorian, and later, alterations in Deansgate and parts of Bradshawgate, the fronts of the houses and shops, the cobbled streets and old paving-stones, the bold cornices, the good brickwork and many other features, all disclose a Classical form which, in the guide-book to a more "historic" city, might be considered worthy of at least an honourable mention.

In Bolton, then, we can see, retaining their influence in spite of the demands of the industrial age, all the qualities which have gone to make the more sophisticated towns of the English Renaissance. The air photograph (fig. 93) makes clear how the criss-cross pattern of streets has been maintained, and figs. 94 and 95 illustrate the characteristics of the streets of smaller houses, and of the "backs"—as the alley-ways behind the main thoroughfares are called. This kind of street scene extended rapidly throughout the early decades of the nineteenth century, forced to absorb earlier groups of industrial and residential buildings and causing the town as a whole to take on a less and less orderly form. It thus becomes more and more difficult, as one moves out from the centre of a town like Bolton—and there are many towns like it in the great complex of the Lancashire textile region alone—to recognise the very beginnings of industrial settlement. But these "beginnings" are still to be found in a thousand little building groups, hidden behind a modern road, or set back from it, and defying the later building-lines; and, by their extensiveness and persistence in the face of attempts to clear them away, they continue to dominate the whole pattern of settlement.

Fig. 93.
Central
Bolton

Fig. 94. Side street in Central Bolton

Fig. 95. An example of "backs", Central Bolton

Fig. 96. Merthyr Tydfil
(O.S. 6″ to mile, 1948)

Fig. 97. Merthyr Tydfil
from the air,
looking west

In South Wales, where towns of generally similar type to those of Lancashire grew up, the early industrial townscape is probably best illustrated by parts of Merthyr Tydfil, that grey, tough town, in the hilly isolation of north Glamorgan. Although Merthyr expanded around an ancient settlement, whose agricultural activities had, since the sixteenth century, been supplemented by iron-smelting in charcoal furnaces, it was still nothing more than a village in the early seventeen-hundreds. Towards the end of the eighteenth century, ironworks using coal were built near Merthyr, and in neighbouring Dowlais, and a rapid increase in population ensued. By 1801, 7,705 people lived in Merthyr, and a continued expansion in the early decades of the nineteenth century raised the figure to 34,977 by 1841. By this time, Merthyr had a population equal to that of Newport, Cardiff and Swansea put together, but its comparative importance declined in the later part of the century.

The shape of Merthyr to-day, in spite of new housing and trading-estates, is largely a reflection of its early industrial character. A great deal of the present form was in existence by 1851, as the Ordnance Survey map of that year shows.[6] At the heart of the town a few narrow and irregular streets follow the lines of those of the medieval village, while beyond this, in seemingly haphazard disposition, are groups of terraced houses, heaps of industrial waste, the derelict land of old ironworks, disused canals, and the relics of Richard Trevithick's first railway system. Yet, preserved in this apparent shapelessness is an old formal street pattern. Merthyr is not, certainly, a town of Renaissance refinement, but it contains, for all that, qualities of style worthy of the label "Classical". The builders of Merthyr possibly did not think of their work as a part of the Georgian tradition of architecture, but their sense of proportion and their occasional stylistic sallies were, as we shall see, none the less Georgian.

Some of the earliest building of the industrial period in Merthyr lies on either side of the River Taff near its main bridging point. It is true that a redevelopment scheme has already caused the demolition of some of the property in this area, and more may have gone by the time these words are in print; nevertheless, since the character of this part of Merthyr is typical of much that may remain elsewhere in the town, and in other industrial areas, for a long time to come, it will be used to illustrate a type of urban landscape that is in a state of considerable flux in present-day Britain.

The street-plan and air photograph of Merthyr (figs. 96 and 97), which show the conditions in about 1948, contain areas of formality and comparative spaciousness. Georgetown, to the west, and Riverside, Bridge Street, and the streets beyond them to the east of the river, do contain a few very narrow lanes, but there is nothing here to compare with the canyon-like courtyards of old Bolton, or the tenements of Glasgow. In its present state much of the oldest housing in Merthyr looks depressing enough, certainly, but this is owing more to dirt and neglect than to the sheer inhumanity of building-design.

Georgetown (named after one of the Crawshay family of ironmasters, and not after the Royal House) is an early housing-estate, built at the junction of hill-slope and valley floor for the workers in the Cyfarthfa Steel Works, originally sited close by.[7] To-day, Georgetown has the air of all those places in our towns classified in planning language as "outworn". It is sad and grimy, with no speck of green in the winter months, when the few thorny trees in the backyards are as black as the great mountain of slag which has transformed the contours of the hill-side, and spread to within a few feet of the cottages themselves. Yet Georgetown is not as totally un-inspired a solution to the problem of housing human beings as is the chess-board of "pre-fabs" perched not far away on a levelled-off bit of the slag heap.[8] Some of the streets in the earlier of these two developments have surprising dignity, and even charm (fig. 98), and the beautiful Pennant sandstone from which the whole estate is largely built is as grand in its massive shapes as the much-admired Cornish granite, and even richer in the variety of its colours.

Fig. 98. "Charm" in Merthyr Tydfil:
Cottages in Georgetown

Throughout Georgetown the houses have the characteristics of Classical buildings in general. The dominant horizontal line and the low pitch of the roof are
strongly marked, as are the well-placed and well-proportioned windows and glazing bars, and the short chimneys. Land, labour and materials were sufficiently
cheap, when Georgetown was built (and the builders were concerned enough for
both architectural proportion and human elbow-room), for each cottage to be given
a fairly generous road frontage, and a little yard or garden, generally at the back.
Outhouses and the walls of the plots are sometimes made of cobbles, presumably
dredged from the river or excavated from its flood plain during the early building
operations, and these add further colour and form to the masonry. The combined
result of all this in Georgetown, and places of similar age in Merthyr, is an urban

scene of long lines of low, crouched, but pleasingly designed buildings of cottage
type (fig. 99). Most of the streets in Georgetown are straight and some are very
wide. Larger buildings are sometimes placed at the end of roads; inns, chapels and
shops, though not methodically sited, have almost without exception a Classical
form. Middle and late Victorian Classical Revival styles have replaced some of the
earliest façades, but the Roman arch "supported" on pilasters, and the cornice
below the line of the low-pitched roof, are commonly retained. The ruthlessly plain
Baptist Chapel in Bethel Street, built in 1815, has a stucco front which was added
some time later, but which is still in the most refined Early Classic style of Welsh
chapel architecture (fig. 100). It might be stretching a point to claim that Nant-y-
Gwenyth Street was intended as a crescent, but the row of cottages which runs
behind it and follows its gentle curve does, at least, have an intimate and friendly
air, not to be despised in the bleak wet climate of the Welsh Hills (fig. 101).

Throughout Merthyr, and its close neighbour Dowlais, and in other mining and
industrial towns of the valleys of Glamorgan and Monmouthshire, the early low
stone terraces, with their occasional pubs and frequent chapels as integral elements,
show a bold and "horizontal" Classical form (fig. 102). In the long streets on the
hill-sides, and in the elongated valley-towns, the oldest buildings are easily distinguished from the taller houses of the late nineteenth century, with red and yellow
brick intrusions around their doors and windows, their high chimney-stacks and
their garden walls. But before this contrasting style became common, the Classical
Revival of the middle of the century was evident in some "better-class" streets, and
in the detached villas of the wealthy. Illustrated again in the Merthyr landscape,
this type of thing is seen east of the High Street, as buildings mount the hill towards
Thomastown (fig. 96). Here is a fairly complete unit of stucco-fronted streets with,
frequently, more imposing buildings on the "chamfered" corner sites. Individually
designed doorways, with porch entrances; moulding around ground-floor windows;

Fig. 99. Rows of Cottages,
Georgetown, Merthyr Tydfil

100. Bethel Chapel, Bethel Street, Merthyr Tydfil

Fig. 101. Nant-y-Gwenyth Street, Merthyr Tydfil

Fig. 102. Riverside, Merthyr Tydfil

sometimes small front gardens, are all features of a still vigorous Classicism. Merthyr's prosperity and the spirit of the Renaissance in British town-building waned together, leaving Classical form of a rudimentary character as a principal legacy in the town to-day.

A close study of Merthyr Tydfil shows that, even within what might be called the Classical Industrial townscape, two clear phases of style can be recognised—the very simple and undecorated building which coincided with the early years of industry, and the slightly more "design-conscious" construction of the second quarter of the nineteenth century.[9] Much more dramatic evidence of such phases, and, at the same time, forceful proof of the esteem in which prevailing architectural taste was held by industrialists who were also humanitarians, is provided by the "model" villages and factories of David Dale at New Lanark and Titus Salt at Saltaire. Coming at the extreme opposite ends of the period of Classical style in industrial town-building, the planned settlements for textile workers which these two manufacturers built are most clear-cut illustrations of the theme of this chapter, and indeed of this book.[10]

David Dale built his village at New Lanark, to draw workers from the Scottish Highlands, in the seventeen-eighties and nineties. His work has been overshadowed by the more socially-significant experiments of Robert Owen on the same site, but he was responsible for the actual building of the mills and the workers' homes in the deep valley of the upper Clyde.[11] Dale was an employer with high principles concerning the quality of the environment in which industry should be carried on; he was also a level-headed businessman aware of the need to make his factory attractive to highlanders leaving their ancient homes for the unknown "south". The massive grandeur of the New Lanark building survives to-day, perfect in almost every detail, and it is not difficult to understand W. Davidson's reference of 1828 to "this beautiful village which has been the admiration of every visitor . . .".[12] Long high terraces of fine stone houses line the steep slopes not far above the tumbling waters of the Clyde. The site is well wooded, rocky and romantic, with splendid soft pastures blanketing the flanks of the hills on either side: it provides a perfect foil for the gaunt but splendid buildings which are so like, and yet so unlike, the slum tenements of Glasgow of slightly later date—now outworn and seemingly forgotten by a society much addicted to talk of town planning (figs. 103, 104 and 105).

Houses and factory buildings in New Lanark have proportions which would not disgrace the streets of an early Renaissance town in Italy. Grand pediments, noble pillared porticoes, great bow-shaped ends of terraces, enhance the nobility of the architecture. The local quarry material, a hard, iron-stained sandstone, has worn to a golden-brown, and the thick, beautiful slate makes a perfect bold capping to the buildings. A church, with a fine bell-tower, forms the central section of a terrace-block (fig. 106). There is great use of massive cast-iron parts for handrails, ladders and whole floors in the factory (which still spins to-day, though nylon and Terylene have taken the place of the original cotton). The whole of this little assemblage of buildings makes, in miniature, a Classical town with the Scottish predilection for height and strength.

Saltaire was the invention of one man—Titus Salt. Like New Lanark, the place stands to-day very much as it did when it was first built, its confident forms surviving in the fine gritstone of the West Riding of Yorkshire. Work began on Salt's factory in 1851. The massive woollen mill—one of the largest of its kind ever built—together with its associated buildings, covered an area of six-and-a-half acres. Its appearance is like that of some vast Classical fortress, and the great chimney, standing by, is an elongated Italian tower. Throughout the eighteen-fifties work proceeded on a town for the factory employees, and on various public buildings including chapels, schools, a library and recreation rooms. All these, together with planned

Fig. 103. New Lanark (after an engraving of c. 1828)

Fig. 104. Factory buildings, New Lanark

Fig. 105. Tenements in present-day Glasgow

Fig. 106.
Church
building,
New Lanark

open spaces and the careful layout of roads and squares, were carried out in a version of the Italianate manner, a style which had been popularised partly by Queen Victoria's Osborne House,[13] and which appealed to many "solid" Yorkshire industrialists. For their period the buildings provided for the workers were particularly fine; in short terraces of two-storied houses, with little gardens at the front, and yards at the back, these were planned as part of an orderly and satisfying design. At the centre and ends of the terraces are taller houses on three floors (these were for the foreman or "overlooker" class), relieving the street of monotony and avoiding the serrated look common to "stepped-down" buildings on sloping sites (fig. 107). All the features of good Classical townscaping are to be found in Saltaire; the street-plan is rectilinear but never tyrannous, since the lines of houses are constantly interrupted by large buildings set back from the normal building line, and the town profile is a pleasing composition of towers, domes and roofs of varied heights. Almost everywhere the round Roman arch is a conspicuous part of the scene, and its use for ground-floor windows in the houses, and at other levels in the public buildings, helps, together with the very low-pitched roofs, to produce a town of emphatic Classicism. Critics have said that, in modern terms, Saltaire is an overcrowded town. But it was designed to be an urban settlement and not a garden village. Its streets could be improved with trees, not, as would be true of many modern estates, because they would hide the buildings, but because of the need for relief from the blackened stone and the grey atmosphere still inseparable from the industrial West Riding. By

Fig. 107. The Church and domestic buildings, Saltaire

almost any standards, Saltaire is a great achievement. As a Classical townscape of the industrial age it is a noble example of a virile style.

The examples of industrial towns that have been studied are but a few of the large number of places which are still characteristic of much of the British urban scene—which, indeed, dominate it in parts of the towns and cities of Wales, Scotland and northern England. Although representing a different social and economic world from that of the towns of leisure and wealth, like Brighton, Cheltenham and Leamington Spa (where the steady refinement of Georgian taste into "Regency" elegance could be applied as much to the design of whole townscapes as to that of dress or furniture), the towns of manufacture and trade were, in a sterner, plainer sense, a reflection of current taste in architecture and town planning. Even the tenements in the Gorbals and other riverside districts of Glasgow owe, in their frontages at least, a modest debt to the Renaissance, as do many buildings in places as far apart as St. Just and Camborne in Cornwall, and Falkirk and Leith in Scotland. In the Black Country and other parts of the Midlands, in spite of massive slum clearances, there still remain the building styles of the early nineteenth century including the characteristic brick cottage of these times with its own kind of charm (fig. 108), but one might be forgiven for refusing to recognise anything beyond expedience in most of the unplanned sprawl west of Birmingham, excelled for shapelessness nowhere else in Britain.

The East End of London has endless examples of townscapes which are counterparts, at a meaner level, of the Georgian metropolis. The qualities of the industrial town which are associated with areas of early heavy industry are not repeated in London, although the main roads leading out of the city on the eastern side were built in a medley of shapes based on the Classical styles of the fine estate-developments farther west. These were the shapes of the houses and small industrial or commercial establishments which made up something very similar to what we know as ribbon-development. This kind of thing survives still, to a great extent, to-day. It seems that, in an area like Bethnal Green for instance, the principal thoroughfares may continue for some time to fulfil the dual functions of shopping-place and principal routeway, and that streets like these may be the last to be replaced in the current phase of rebuilding which is going on around them (fig. 109). As the built-up area continued to increase, throughout the early years of the nineteenth century, the enlarging demands of the great capital led to the setting up, haphazardly, in the wedges of land between the main roads, of that assortment of establishments necessary to satisfy the needs of a metropolis—for example, brickworks, market gardens and breweries—while in all the remaining lands, wherever space was available for the terrace-rows of workers' houses, the London version of the Industrial townscape emerges and is again, for all its reduction to the barest outlines of Classicism as in Brick Lane (fig. 110), instantly recognisable as of Georgian origin.

Fig. 108. Brick cottage, Leicester

Fig. 110. Brick Lane, Bethnal Green

Fig. 109. Bethnal Green Road, London

Fig. 111.
Birmingham
Art Gallery
and Town H
(far right)

Postscript to the Industrial Towns

Prior to, and in the early part of, Queen Victoria's reign, the already great and still expanding industrial cities built for themselves monumental public buildings, and sometimes whole city centres, in the Classical style. These are currently receiving increasing attention as architectural achievements (in time, it may be hoped, to save most of them from the demolition squad). Birmingham Town Hall was already complete by 1835, and was based on the style of a Roman temple, and the neighbouring Art Gallery is a contrasting Baroque (fig. 111); Leeds Town Hall, also temple-like, with the addition of a domed tower, was started in 1853; St. George's Hall, Liverpool, was finished in 1854, and, together with the fine civic buildings in its vicinity, forms a monumental if somewhat limited town-centre.

As a genuine attempt to plan a central area, and thus to build very extensively in a Classical urban style, the finest example from this period is undoubtedly the Newcastle of John Dobson. Employed to carry out the plan of the building-magnate Richard Grainger, Dobson helped to design ". . . nine streets . . . including . . . a theatre, a dispensary, a music-hall, a lecture room, a company's hall, two chapels, two auction-marts, ten inns, twelve public-houses, four banks, forty first-class private houses and three hundred and twenty-five houses with shops".[14] Most of the work was done in the eighteen-thirties and forties, and now, over a hundred years later, where some few of the buildings have been cleaned to a creamy ochre, they demonstrate the true splendour as well as the magnificent scale of this piece of town-building. Much of central Newcastle is still black, even by the standards of English industrial towns: strung with trolley-bus wires and covered with mine-dust, the town must still make do with such adjectives as "tough", "robust", and "rugged" to describe its urban landscape. But given a thorough face-lift, and the guarantee of a genuinely smokeless zone, its central area could be one of the most beautiful in Britain (fig. 112).

Fig. 112. Central Newcastle with Grey's Monument

8. *Transitional Town Styles*

THE story of design in town-building is one of overlapping phases, rather than of clearly separated periods, but these phases represent the recurrent expression of a few basic preferences. In Britain to-day, a town whose foundation precedes the year 1850 will contain, for certain, some inheritance of Classical form, and some of Romantic style. These two elements are the main threads in the pattern of architectural shapes in our towns, closely interwoven and sometimes almost indistinguishable from one another, but each, from time to time, emerging as the chief component.

Romantic notions of design in individual buildings survived the eighteenth century (as was shown in Chapter 4), and were coming into favour by the early part of the nineteenth century. Many well-known architects, who normally worked in the Classical manner, produced Gothic and other Romantic designs for wealthy and strong-minded patrons. Augustus Pugin, employed at first as a draughtsman by John Nash, became the prophet of Gothic Revivalism, and with his book *Contrasts*, published in 1836, he pleaded for a return of steeply-pitched roofs, revealed gables and soaring steeples—in fact of the complete medieval scene (fig. 113). Amongst the architects of churches and other public buildings—notably town halls—there followed a vigorous conflict of opinion; some (especially those with ecclesiastical commissions) favoured the rising, aspiring and highly decorated forms of English and Continental Gothic building, while others returned ever more assiduously to the Greek and Roman prototypes for the framework of a new Classic Revival. Even individual buildings contained at times a double element, and Bannister Fletcher says of Sir Charles Barry's Westminster Palace (1840–60) (which forms perhaps the finest piece of architecture related to an urban site in Britain) "... symmetry of plan, simplicity of idea, and richness of character pervades the design, which is Classic in inspiration, Gothic in clothing ...".[1]

Town-building throughout the nineteenth century was necessarily influenced by this "Battle of Styles", and as the Romantic Movement gained ground, under the influence of developments in literature, art and music, there was a slow but steady swing away from the Classical manner of treating the more prosaic, as well as the more dramatic, urban features. But builders of town-houses for the middle classes, and of terraces of humble dwellings for the workers, were not easily to be won over to what was, after all, very much an "avant-garde" movement. The

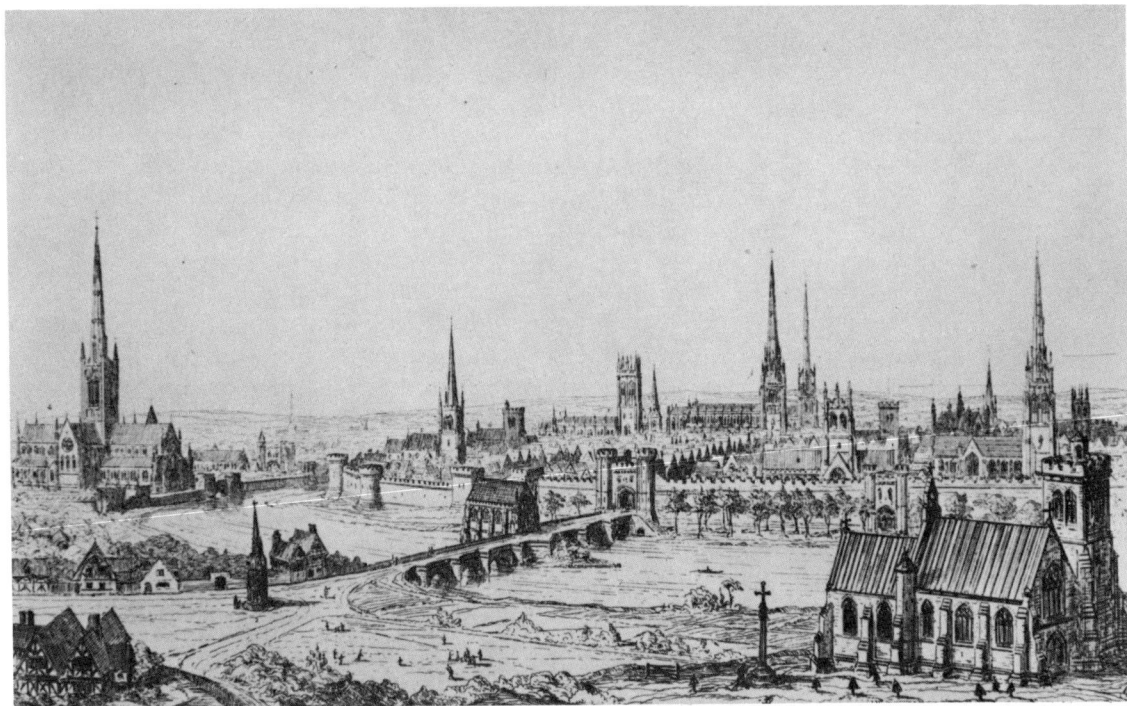

Fig. 113. "Catholic town in 1440". Augustus Pugin's idealisation of a Medieval town, from his original drawing

exponents of the Gothic style must have been viewed, by the average speculative builder and his client in the nineteenth century, in much the same way as the work of Frank Lloyd Wright and Le Corbusier is viewed by the same parties at the present time. For the most part, the middle decades of Victoria's reign, as far as the principal towns and the growing industrial cities were concerned, was a period of compromise, even of uncertainty, with much emphasis still on the well-tried formulae of the Classical townscape. For almost fifty years after Pugin's appeal, and in spite of the urgent championing of the Gothic Revival by the great Victorian writer and critic, John Ruskin, domestic architecture, in its siting, proportion and detail, still leaned heavily on the Renaissance, while edging forward, with current taste, in the use of bay windows, the gradual steepening of roof-pitch, and the more adventurous use of materials. Meanwhile, in the second half of the nineteenth century, architects of major buildings abandoned the "Gothic v. Greek and Roman" stylistic contest, and built in an extravagant mixture of borrowed styles, making the choice for the small builder an increasingly difficult one.

115

The kind of building that was typical of good-class residential developments in mid-century is illustrated well in Torquay. The aerial view of part of the south coast resort (fig. 114) shows villa-estates on either side of the Torwood Valley, which leads down to the harbour and main urban nucleus of the seaside town. These estates of private houses are spread out over steep and well-wooded hill-sides, though it must be remembered that the fine matured gardens, including many exotic trees, and the curving roads lined with splendid stone walls, are later additions to the original scene. Nevertheless, in the choice of site and in the individual design of each villa there is clear desire to have done with the terrace and the crescent and the crowded built-up town. It is in the comparatively regular placing of the houses (seen best in the air photograph) and in the preponderant choice of the Italianate style for individual houses, that the Classical fights a well-matched battle with its friendly rival, the Romantic.

Torquay experienced its first major building boom, as a resort for wealthy invalids and holiday-makers, in the middle decades of the nineteenth century. A good deal of terrace-building and the first stages of villa-construction had been completed by the time the railway reached the town in 1848. Although a very considerable road journey separated the town from the metropolis, Torquay was by no means out of touch with prevailing fashions in architecture. Percy Russell says that the Gothic Revival had set in strongly, in Torquay, in the "mid-forties"—"several years before Ruskin wrote his *Seven Lamps of Architecture*".[2] Gothic villas of this early date are scattered on the hill-sides amongst the other splendid domestic architecture of this beautifully-sited town, but the favourite style of the eighteen-forties and eighteen-fifties was undoubtedly that borrowed from Italy. Now, however, it was not the temple, basilica, or city palace, but the later country or suburban residence that was chosen as a pattern, and the irregular masses produced by asymmetrically placed towers, gables and wings was an indication of the Victorian preference for Romantic arrangement even when Classical details were being used. Although an excellent building-stone was quarried near at hand in the beds of Devonian limestone, it was only in the Gothic building that its colour and texture were preferred to the stucco which covered it in the Italianate houses. The surface features of the majority of villas in the Warberry Hill and Lincombe Hill Drives, and in the more closely-built streets of Torre, where the slightly less wealthy buyer found smaller sites near the railway, add up to townscapes of superficial resemblance to those of Mediterranean Rivieras (figs. 115 and 116).

The common failure to see much good in the towns of the second half of the nineteenth century is largely due to their association with industrialism, and we should now turn to a town built almost wholly at this time. Middlesbrough was a boom-town of the nineteenth century, and to-day is a record of the notions which prevailed, in about the eighteen-sixties and eighteen-seventies, of how to plan and design extensive urban sites for industrial workers. From 1850 to 1900, in response to the needs of the iron industry, Middlesbrough's population rose from 7,431 to 91,302. An urban revolution perforce accompanied the industrial one, and regiments of terrace-houses were built close to the ironworks and the new railway. A

Fig. 114. A vertical view of
villa-development in Torquay

Fig. 115. Villas, Torre, Torquay

Fig. 116. A townscape of villas, Torre

public park separated this part of the town from sites favoured by the prosperous middle class, while the early nucleus, near the station, contained the chief public and commercial buildings. The street map of Middlesbrough to-day is a dramatic and seemingly indelible testimony to the energy of an age and to a ruthlessly simplified conception of the meaning of the word "town" (fig. 117).

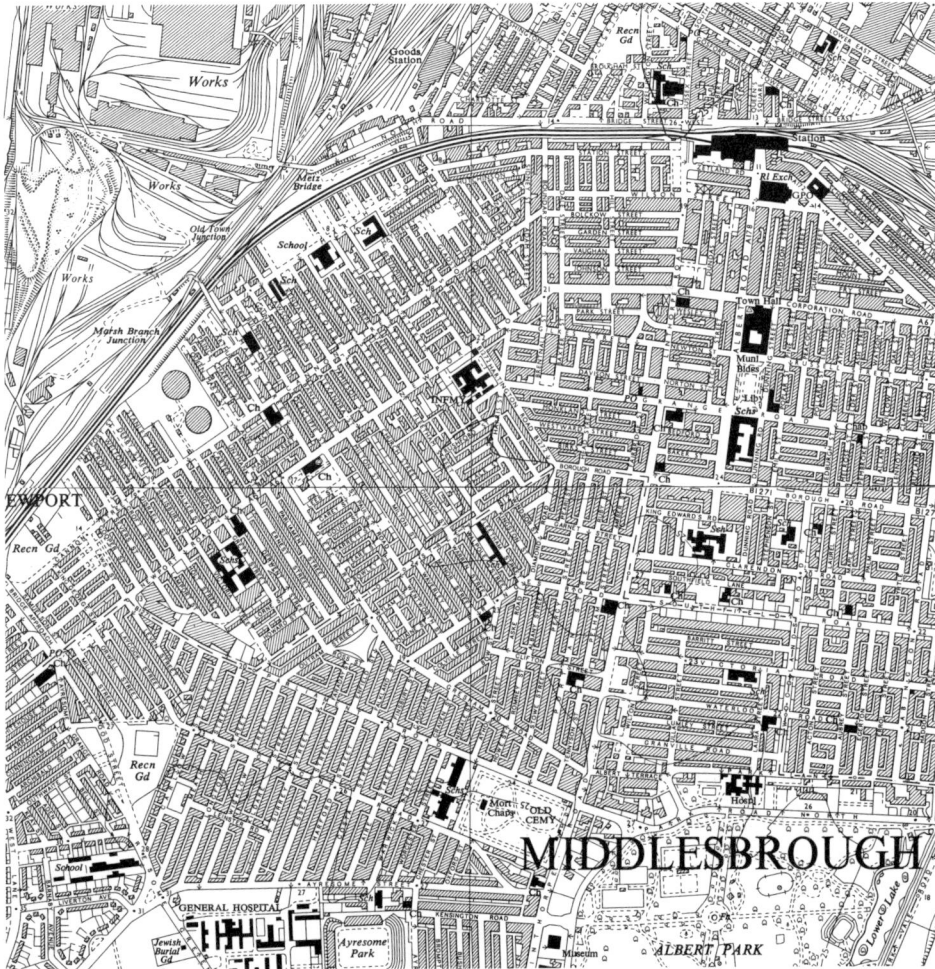

Fig. 117.
Part of the O.S. 6″ to the mile map of Middlesbrough, 1954

Fig. 118. Terraces in the Newport district
of Middlesbrough

It is customary to regard the long rows of houses of the industrial workers of Middlesbrough, and other towns or town-regions of this period, as the epitome of functional building: the layout of the street patterns, too, in such places, is taken to represent the nadir of town planning ideas. Asa Briggs, in his book *Victorian Cities*, quotes some words which sum up the very proper moral judgment which several generations of reformers have used to rebuke the meanness of our industrial cities; in building its "rows and rows of little brown streets", Middlesbrough, said Lady Bell, "cannot wait to consider anything else but time and space".[3] Yet this is not entirely true. The stiff, gridded system of the Middlesbrough streets is not different in essence from the plans of most deliberately projected cities throughout history. The rows of houses exhibit characteristics of period style, and each row is marked out in some way from its neighbours by variation in the treatment of brickwork, or in the shape and decoration of the framework of doors and windows. In some of the earliest surviving streets, near the station, the doorways of houses are trimmed in wood with a Classical architrave supported on piers in the form of simplified pilasters, while in streets of a slightly later date, emphasis is removed from the house-entrance (not for the sake of total economy, but probably because even architects were doing away with the portico as a principal feature of their major buildings), and placed instead on lintels of windows and doors, string-courses in coloured brick, brick cornices, and other details. These little, confused attempts to give the streets something of the mode of building-design that prevailed in more favoured places, pathetic as they may seem now beneath their cloak of grime, are not so very different from methods used by present-day architects to give identity to the streets and "neighbourhoods" of housing estates and New Towns, by such means as variations of the surface texture of walls, and a liberal distribution of the colours of the spectrum in the paintwork of front doors.

The Newport district of Middlesbrough, which was developed after 1860, shows particularly well the dilemma of mid-Victorian designers of multiple housing-blocks, who must have been dimly conscious of the collapse of the Classical style, and the revival of preference for medieval shapes. The illustration (fig. 118) shows five blocks of dwellings in this part of the town as they are seen to-day from a site from which older streets have been cleared. At first glance this is just another group

Fig. 119. Lime Street, Middlesbrough

Fig. 120. Street plan to the west of New Town, Edinburgh (O.S. map 6″ to mile, 1956)

of parallel rows of boxes placed end to end—an elementary solution to an elementary problem. But these houses are different from the houses built in Merthyr Tydfil—and elsewhere—in the early days of the Industrial Revolution; they are taller, their roofs are more steeply pitched, their chimneys are longer, and their façades are decorated in the manner of the time. Above each door in Lime Street, and giving it a striking identity, stone-carved heads with crowns, locally known as the "Kings and Queens", have been set as key-stones and are reminiscent of medieval gargoyles (fig. 119). It would require a distorted imagination to call these houses an example of the Romantic Movement in domestic architecture, but they do show a leaning towards some medieval shapes. In Middlesbrough we seem to be looking at the very antithesis of the Romantic townscape towards which many architects and designers had already aspired, and yet a comparison with Saltaire will show the extent of the change that had taken place since the turn of the half-century.

In our larger towns and cities mid-Victorian times produced a great "explosion" of middle-class terrace-housing. A late phase of development in the "New Town" area of Edinburgh has left a fine record of this period of building. Not as famed as the original streets and squares of the eighteenth-century plan to the north of Princes Street, the crescents and gardens west of Shandwick Place are, in their own way, splendid pieces of urban design (fig. 120). Grosvenor Crescent, facing Lansdowne Crescent across a characteristically lozenge-shaped and well-wooded private garden, was built from 1869 to 1870 (fig. 121). The unity and simplicity of façade achieved in Georgian building by continuous string-courses and cornices, as well as the horizontality created by these features, have been partly replaced by the strong vertical lines and deeply sculptured effect of the bay windows. The chimneys, too, are fairly tall and are not hidden from the street by the parapet as they are more often in earlier parts of the New Town. Yet there are still Classical elements in the scene, and in spite of the thrusting spires of St. Mary's Church, in which the Gothic Revival is so unreservedly marked, the balustrade, running boldly along the top of the façade of the crescent, and the similar feature which crowns each bay, record, if rather stolidly, an era that was passing away.

The type of building represented so well by Grosvenor Crescent, Edinburgh, is repeated over extensive areas of our cities and towns, and records a period of rapid urban growth at the height of Victorian industrial and commercial prosperity. Sometimes, for the very well-off, buildings were detached, especially in "holiday" towns and the grander new suburbs, but this phase, like the preceding one under the Georges, was one in which houses and public buildings often gave straight on to the public thoroughfare, or were, at most, separated from it by a narrow "area", or small open space. Here building density was high, and the sense of a closely-knit urban community was not lost, in spite of the steady drawing apart, in both location and wealth, of the employers and the employed.

Fig. 121.
Grosvenor
Crescent,
Edinburgh

All the larger British cities contain extensive survivals from this time. In Glasgow, in early Victorian times, building in the areas north-west of the city's centre continued the tradition of rectangular blocks similar to the courtyard-tenements of the Gorbals. But by mid-century the fronts of these blocks had become more ornate, with bay windows, sometimes corbelled, and with taller chimneys than hitherto, as the spread of development reached out to the banks of the Kelvin River, and sometimes the blocks themselves gave way to terraces and crescents (figs. 122 and 123). By the early eighteen-sixties the area around Park Circus had been built up in styles very similar to those of Grosvenor Crescent and its neighbourhood in Edinburgh, and, twenty years later, the roads to the north of the Botanical Gardens had been completed. Botanic Crescent and Kelvin Drive, overlooking the Kelvin River (fig. 124), illustrate the Victorian approach to planning near parks and important physical features, and show, in contrast to the Classical townscape, an enjoyment of the irregular curves that derive from nature. Victorian parks, also shown in fig. 124, make a subject of study in themselves: they are essentially a part of the townscape of the period, and are often far ahead of their time in their convincing handling of the Romantic elements of design.

The West End estates of London were succeeded, in a north-westerly direction, by townscapes very similar in general character to those which have been described in the two chief Scottish cities. Here, there was a veritable landscape of buildings in styles ever less mindful of Classical requirements, and increasingly inclined towards the "broken" lines created by successions of bay windows, and the varied textures that can be created by using brick, stucco and stone in composing the face of a street. Beyond Paddington, in the direction of Kensal Green, early Victorian Classical façades, with rather elaborate detail in the moulding of stucco, give way to surfaces of yellow-brick facings between mouldings which are left around doors and windows: and then, still farther out, as in the Glasgow succession, bay windows, steeper roofs and taller chimneys—in terraces and crescents where red brick often becomes the favourite building material—provide more examples of the mid- and late-Victorian, "half-way house".

Almost any journey out of central London to the north, west and south will pass through areas of the kind just described. Mostly these areas of towns are neglected to-day as they are no longer in demand as well-to-do residential areas. At the same time they are well enough built to resist decay, even when treated in the most ruthless fashion; they are expensive to demolish, too, and, although on valuable land, their sites have not yet acquired the inflated values of central areas. They therefore represent one of the most pressing problems for those concerned with the question of town maintenance, and it is to be regretted that the many fine qualities of these townscapes are so little appreciated.

The extensive areas of towns that were built of red-brick terraces as the nineteenth century nears its close are still very much with us to-day. Much development at this time came under the influence of various Acts of Parliament which were aimed at improving working-class housing conditions, and these acts resulted in what has come to be known in many of our cities as "by-law" housing, since it was subject to local regulation of such things as the width of streets, the provision of water-supply and sanitation, and the allowance made for light and ventilation.

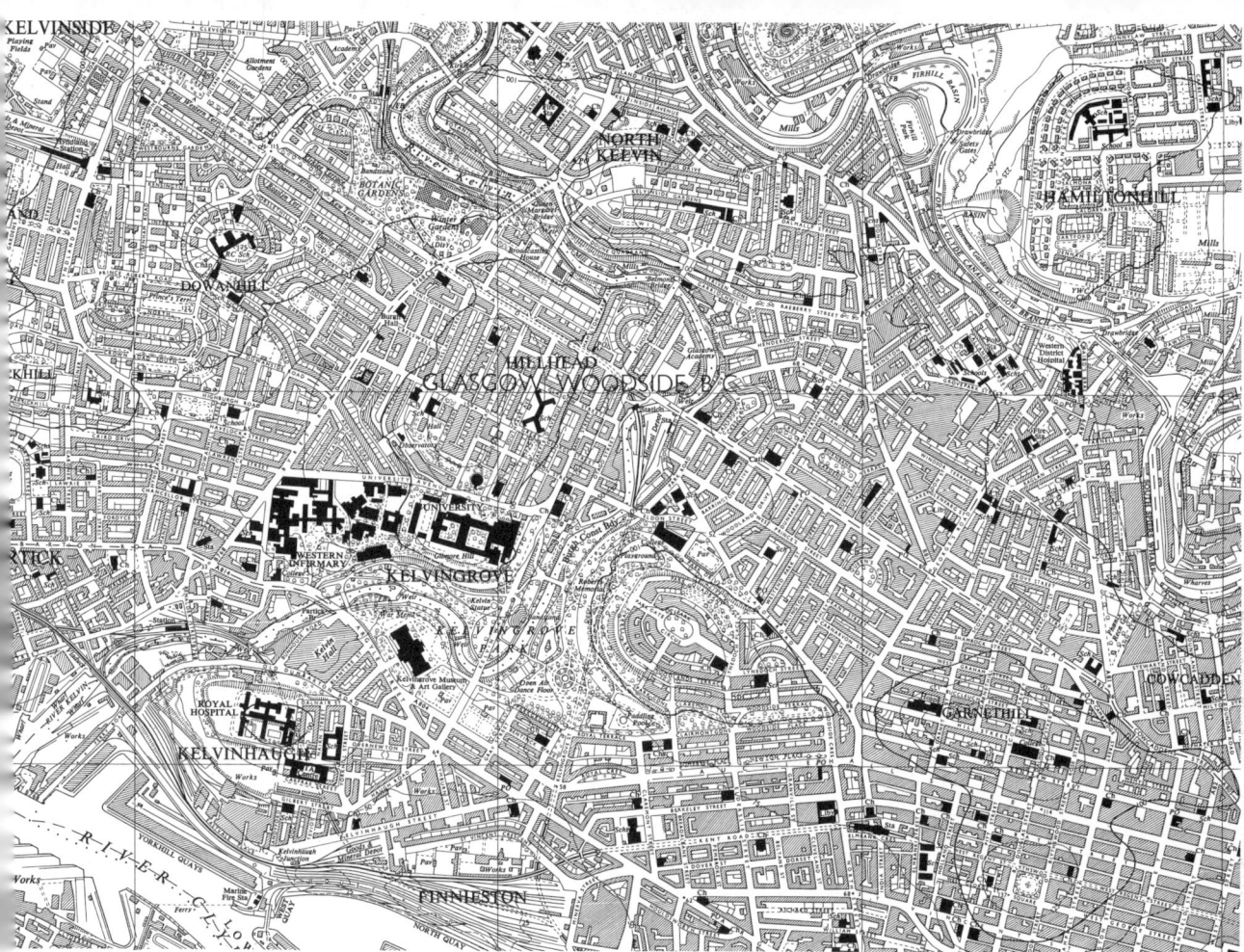

Fig. 122. Part of the O.S. map 6″ to the mile of Glasgow, 1956

Fig. 123. Streets of Glasgow, west of the city centre

Fig. 124. Botanic Gardens and nearby housing, Glasgow

Fig. 125. The roofs of Openshaw

Areas like those described in Middlesbrough are of this type, and they can be found all over northern and central England, surviving to-day because they are not such unhealthy places to live in as were the many overcrowded regions, dating from the early years of industrialism, which fringed the city centres. The great mass of streets of hideous terraces which still make up so much of Salford, and other parts of the Manchester conurbation, are hard to reconcile with any idea of a sense of design, but it is possible to see, if we can temporarily suspend our faculties for criticising the in-humanity of the present condition of these places, the almost despairing attempt to raise the roofs into a Gothic pitch, and to point the chimneys skywards, in the picture of the houses of Openshaw in fig. 125.

Some townscapes which date from this period have had a more fortunate geographical situation than others in which to exist during the chequered years of the twentieth century. Streets similar to those of Openshaw spread in their hundreds around our medium-sized ports, as well as around the great industrial towns, and in the former the usually cleaner air of the district and the modest scale and compact character of the urban structure have led to something rather more tolerable for purposes of human occupation. Towns like Barrow-in-Furness, Hull and Portsmouth are dominated by the form of the town-building which occurred in the last decades of the nineteenth century. Barry, the Glamorganshire coal-port, is another excellent example of the period, since it was built in one short phase—around the turn of the century—on a previously unoccupied site.

Apart from one or two hamlets, the area which came to be occupied by the port of Barry was uninhabited in the early eighteen-eighties. In response to the need for increased facilities for the export of coal, and for servicing steamships—since Cardiff was proving quite inadequate for coping with this trade—the building of Barry Docks began in 1884. Unlike our contemporary New Towns, which are planned to provide a variety of employment, Barry—a product of individual commercial zeal—was built to serve the one need of handling coal for transhipment. The sloping land which lies in a wide arc, facing the docks and the Bristol Channel, became transformed by acres of little pale-grey and red houses, built mainly in

brick, but sometimes in the Liassic limestone of the district. In twenty years, from 1885 to 1905, the bulk of the town was built, and the simple form of its terraces and very occasional detached villas is clearly shown on the Ordnance Survey map of the town for 1914 (fig. 126). The building which had been completed by the time this map was drawn was not quite as uninspired as the plan of the streets would suggest. Solidly constructed houses and good gardens with stone or brick walls were the rule, and there is evidence everywhere of a conscientious endeavour to provide "decent" places for workpeople. Street after street displays slight variation in style and one is compelled to feel that these variations are a direct reflection of the divi-

Fig. 126. Barry, Glamorgan: from 6″ to the mile O.S. map of 1914

sions of social class. The simplest of these styles are in the poorer streets where lime-stone is sometimes used for the front walls of houses, and a straight line of eaves gives an almost Classical look to the terraces (fig. 127). Elsewhere, as land and house values increase, so does the quantity of brick decoration and the number of bay windows, gables, decorative front-garden walls and the like, though the level of good taste is not necessarily enhanced by these additions (fig. 128).

Half a century has gone by since the 1914 map of Barry was drawn, and very little has changed in the principal parts of the built-up area. The fresh prevailing winds from the south-west, blowing off the Bristol Channel, kept the dock coal-dust away from the town in the early days. After the depression of the 1930's the port ceased to do much business in coal, and so there is little of the usual grime of the industrial town to prevent us seeing, in Barry, the form, colour and quality of building which was characteristic of so much townscape in the late nineteenth and early twentieth centuries.

Fig. 127. Queen Street, Barry

Throughout this chapter, a townscape has been described which was created at a time when very little thought was given to the good looks of the urban environment. It is no use trying to disguise the fact that most of the building of this period consists of monotonous, straight streets of houses in styles not clearly committed to any tradition or formal principle. Yet even the worst of these areas—in the industrial districts—were still well-enough built to be serviceable to-day, and may long remain to represent what we know as "twilight housing". Of course there are some good things to observe even here: for example the red bricks of the period—generally laid in pleasing traditional bonds—which are not all of uniform colour and unpleasant glazed texture. As they now show signs of maturing, some of these bricks wear a warm rusty glow that is not so very different from the lovely colours of seventeenth-century houses. But for our main purpose, the significance of this transitional period of urban design is that it shows the tension which existed between the Classical and the Romantic currents at the end of the nineteenth century, and we turn, in the two chapters which follow, to look at a new and more positive phase in the evolution of British town design.

Fig. 128. Terrace houses, Barry

9. *Romantic Town Scenery*

WHILE the dying fire of Classicism in town-building smoked on into the twentieth century, the last quarter of the nineteenth experienced an uprising of the forces favouring Romantic design in architecture. The Romantic townscape which eventually appeared, and which dominated the first few decades of the present century, was not only an architectural concept but also an expression of preference for (or at least of a fairly willing acceptance of) a certain kind of semi-urban environment on the part of the large number of occupants of new private and local authority houses. Architects and builder-speculators of the type that had produced large town-estates for the gentry and the men of big business found less and less custom for this type of work as the nineteenth century neared its close. Instead, builders working on a much smaller scale, and visionaries of the Town Planning Movement (who, though they were mainly concerned with social progress, were far from indifferent to aesthetic considerations) helped to direct the style of building in towns.

To what extent client or designer is responsible for the ultimate product of their partnership is a highly debatable issue: both helped to produce the Georgian and early Victorian towns on the one hand, and the suburban areas of more recent times on the other. But whereas, in the period since the beginnings of the Renaissance and prior to the time of large-scale attempts to improve the condition of the mass of working-class people, architect and patron must always have paid special regard to prevailing trends in taste, and both must have thought of "style" as something distinct from function and as a part of a valued artistic tradition, most of the builders and buyers of late Victorian Britain must have been aware of taking part in a social revolution as well as an artistic one. The notion that form should spring from function was newly in the air; so was the belief that the function of building was to provide a decent home in privacy and semi-rural surroundings for a large mass of the people. These ideas produced, in Britain, a solution which now seems characteristically British—the Garden City (the prototype of the Romantic townscape). This development, and, more particularly, the garden suburbs which followed in its wake, have sometimes been mistakenly described as evidence of a decline in taste. It is really a change of a different order. Popular taste now came to replace specialised taste, as popular need replaced specialised need, as the main town-building force. To British townscape the importance of this period of development cannot be over-emphasised, for not only does it contribute a major geographical area to our towns (a far greater one than that of any of the previous townscapes discussed) but it may well be argued that it is this period which establishes on a significant scale, for the first time since the Middle Ages, a truly indigenous urban style. (In addition to criticism of a purely aesthetic kind of the towns that

Fig. 129. The Red House, Upton, Kent

now began to grow, there is the more complex one of those who consider the stress on medieval village styles of this period an irrelevance, and an attempt to escape from the facts of industrial and city life. A new development altogether, profoundly affecting method and style in building, was taking place at the same time as the growth of the Romantic town. This, originating partly in the work of the engineers —especially the railway and bridge-builders of the mid-nineteenth century—was assisted by the movement in visual art towards abstraction. The architecture and townscape which result from this development will be studied in a later chapter.)

The beginnings of the British Romantic townscape are to be found in the movements which championed Gothic and other medieval forms in architecture, and which have already been described. Pugin's "Christian Gothic" had immense influence on subsequent church building, though it never multiplied into his hoped-for Gothic town. Ruskin's crusade in favour of Venetian and other Italian medieval models, and for "truth to nature" in art, was infectious and influenced public buildings, business premises, private villas and so on, though it did not directly lead to a new town-form. Taken together with other developments in the arts, the work of these two men produced fertile ground, in which the ideas of William Morris and the schemes of such practical planners as Ebenezer Howard and George Cadbury could take root and grow. Morris not only followed Ruskin as a champion of the Gothic Revival but also set about designing for himself—chiefly furniture, fabrics and wallpapers—in highly original adaptations from medieval sources. His ideas, as they apply to buildings, are probably best seen in the famous Red House of Upton, Kent (fig. 129), which was designed for him by Philip Webb (and built in 1859–60) and which clearly influenced a great amount of subsequent domestic architecture. Of this house John Gloag says: "It possessed an emotional appeal; it had a romantic originality, and the architect's skilful use of red brick and tiles led to the rediscovery of texture".[1] But the Red House was far ahead of its time and it was many years before large parts of towns came to be built in styles derived from Webb and Morris; this change awaited the encouragement of the developers both of small middle-class private estates, in city suburbs, and of the model villages and "Garden Cities" in places like Bournville and Letchworth.

Building in the more expensive suburbs of the large cities, and in the inland resorts and seaside towns favoured in the last decades of Victoria's reign and in the first part of Edward's, was becoming increasingly Romantic. Whereas in Torquay in the eighteen-fifties and sixties Italianate villas (described in Chapter 8) predominated over the houses in Gothic styles, in such places as Scarborough and Harrogate, in the eighties and nineties, the number of houses owing their form to various medieval prototypes outweighs that of buildings with Classical connections, and the former group survives to become important parts of these towns to-day.

Harrogate has, in its central areas, fine examples of mid-Victorian buildings which help to maintain a closely built-up feeling. Crescents and terraces are seen to excellent advantage right in the heart of the spa, set off by expanses of handsome public gardens. But, since the growth of the town continued steadily right up to the end of the Edwardian era, the character of the urban design, beyond the core, in the inner suburban zones, is a good example of the early Romantic townscape. Here the areas of development are of two kinds; one is made up of rows of terrace-houses (usually of brick with Tudor features) and similar to those of the towns studied in the last chapter, the other is formed from detached villas along wide, curving drives. This second type, an example not of an intentionally planned "garden suburb", but of the highly individual taste and exclusiveness characteristic of the well-to-do classes of the period, shows how the picturesque style of building had, by the end of the nineteenth century, finally won a complete victory over formality of design.

Fig. 130.
Part of a map of
Harrogate, showing
the date of buildings
in the central area
(after J. A. Patmore)

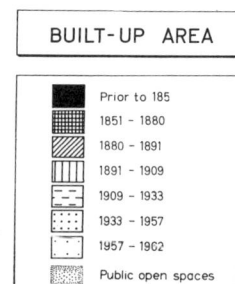

BUILT-UP AREA

	Prior to 185
	1851 – 1880
	1880 – 1891
	1891 – 1909
	1909 – 1933
	1933 – 1957
	1957 – 1962
	Public open spaces

Fig. 131. The Cairn Hotel, Ripon Road, Harrogate

Fig. 132. Scene in the
Canongate, Edinburgh

The area of Harrogate directly to the north of Valley Gardens was built in the years between 1891 and 1909 (fig. 130). Detached from both town centre and working-class districts, yet within easy reach of both (as "guide-book language" might put it) the houses in Clarence Drive, York Road, Duchy Road, etc., may be thought of as either large and very individual versions of picturesque cottages, or small samples of Romantic villas. They are built in a fine gritstone, the sombre grey of which is relieved by the liberal use of decorative window-frames, doorways and porches, balconies and verandas and elaborate barge-boarding, all in painted wood. The Cairn Hotel in Ripon Road is a massive example of the same kind of thing, which, though its architectural style is not in favour to-day, should be compared with a medieval town scene such as the one in the Canongate, Edinburgh (figs. 131 and 132), if the intentions of the designer are to be appreciated. Other villas of this part of Harrogate (fig. 133) have qualities not to be despised. Fretted, serrated, and vertically elongated shapes are common at this time in all classes of building, and they are features which are found well developed in parts of another Yorkshire town—Scarborough.

Fig. 133. Edwardian Villas, Harrogate

Fig. 134. Scarborough from the air

Seen from the air, a large part of the street-plan of Scarborough echoes the flowing lines of this part of the coast of the East Riding (fig. 134). Even the early streets and public paths, built at or just before the beginning of the nineteenth century, show a graceful mingling of the town and its natural setting, and, as the century advanced, apart from a few very formal street "grids" and such Classical building as the vast and Baroque Grand Hotel, a seemingly instinctive irregularity of layout was made to extend inland from the promenades and cliff-drives, as development spread up the curving valleys and over the rolling land between them.

Valley Road, following a fairly deep and winding cleft behind South Bay, mounts from the sea front through a well-wooded park towards the residential building beyond. In its upper part it is lined with tall, fairly closely-packed houses, built in the early years of the present century (fig. 135). Although this part of Scarborough is largely built in a yellow brick of rather harsh hue, and lacks the spacious air of the best parts of Edwardian Harrogate, the building styles have all the variety and the sense of abandonment of tradition that is associated with the best residential development of the period: and, for all their pretentiousness, these styles attempt an air of rusticity like that of a house in fictitious "Newborough" described by Osbert Sitwell in these rather acid terms:

"It was such a comfortable house, and had such a 'nice' garden, too, on the other side—quite like being in the country. It was difficult to imagine, when one was in it, that one was in a town. The garden, edged with split-oak palings, was full of speckled laurel-bushes and dirty evergreens, graced in the spring by the spidery, thin mauve flowers of a few Indian lilacs, the dying fireworks of a laburnum tree with a hollow in its centre which had at one time been filled with cement, and later by a few perfectly correct but rather scentless roses."[2]

All our principal towns, and especially the resorts of the well-to-do, added to their extent at this time by means of high-class residences of the type that have just been described. In the far south of the country Bournemouth (whose character is perhaps more completely dominated by the effects of this period on the wealthier urban scene than is that of any other place in England) also illustrates many of the features associated with the development of towns in late Victorian times.

Fig. 135.
Houses in
Valley Road,
Scarborough

Everywhere medieval styles became increasingly popular—in the homes for industrial workers (when something more than minimum consideration was given to the domestic needs of this class) as well as in areas occupied by the rich. Exceptionally good examples of these two types of Romantic urban building may be illustrated from two widely separated parts of the kingdom—in Bedford Park, Chiswick, and in the textile workers' cottages of Dunfermline. The former was the work of Norman Shaw—one of the most influential architects in the London of the last decades of the nineteenth century. Though he built in a variety of "revived" styles, his part in the Bedford Park town planning experiment at Chiswick showed a striking use of lines and shapes which, for all their association with English and Dutch styles of the seventeenth century, are intended to create a Romantic scene. In the late eighteen-seventies Norman Shaw, with other architectural assistance, executed a plan of a Mr. Jonathan T. Carr for "the construction of an artistic suburb which was called Bedford Park".[3] To-day this tiny suburb is impressive in its maturity. Wide roads, with tree-lined, broad sidewalks, and wooden fences or shrubberies edging the front gardens, set off the tall, mellow buildings. The highly original versions of Dutch-gabled and Queen Anne villas, sometimes in pairs, are well built, and are carefully sited to gain the maximum informality (given the straightforward road plan and the limited number of designs of the houses themselves). Tile-hung upper stories and sections of gables are particularly well arranged, and these, together with the rich-looking bricks in various shades of red and yellow, and some stucco, make a fine medley of colours. The lack of garage space is, now, a grave weakness of the scheme, but much of the good quality of Bedford Park comes from the close grouping of the buildings which is achieved without ever suggesting overcrowding. Indeed, a friendly "village" quality seems to have been crossed with one of urban scale (fig. 136).

Fig. 136.
A road at
Bedford Park,
Turnham
Green,
London

Fig. 137. Working-class cottages, Dunfermline

Bedford Park is certainly a fine example of conscious informality and Romanticism in town-building. It was very "advanced" for its time and came close to realising, in a small way, William Morris's ideal of an environment designed and executed by artist-craftsmen. It was not the fault of Morris, Webb and Shaw that a social revolution was about to break out and spread poor imitations of their architectural ideas across Britain. The sort of towns which they would have liked to see called for the rich and complex compositions of a rare creative imagination. Not surprisingly, society in the declining years of Queen Victoria's reign was not ready to give the requisite powers to the few who might have possessed the ability to design an environment for a whole nation of town dwellers.

In the Scottish textile town of Dunfermline a small area of workers' cottages was laid out in the eighteen-nineties. The streets here are wide and the houses are of one and two stories, the latter sometimes having the large dormer window so popular in parts of Scotland. The good grey-stone construction, and the human scale and simple cottage-like proportions, give an air of almost rural calm to this very industrial quarter, and are a reminder that the last years of the nineteenth century were not devoid of instances of good building in working-class areas (fig. 137).

The examples of town building styles so far studied in this chapter show the private developer still at work, forced now to move farther and farther out from the central areas of the cities and largest towns, and less and less, both in style and scale, concerned with great enterprises of civic design. There was, of course, at the same time a great deal of alteration to the appearance of principal streets in cities and towns by the rebuilding, on individual sites, of shops, banks and other business premises—usually contrasting with those of previous periods in their increased height, their varied use of texture and materials, and their mixing of Classical and Romantic elements. But the chief contribution of this period to a really comprehensive Romantic townscape, and certainly the one which survives most convincingly to-day, comes from the work of the Garden City builders.

The social and economic importance of the well-known settlements of Bournville, Port Sunlight and the Rowntree village at New Earswick, together with the fact that their architectural design is the reverse of the monumental, have overshadowed the contribution that these places make to the English urban landscape. George Cadbury built Bournville as an attempted solution to overcrowding in the industrial areas of Birmingham, and was as much concerned with the provision of community buildings, open spaces, recreational facilities and the like as he was with the quality of individual houses. The contrast between the smoke-enthralled streets of Birmingham and the Black Country on the one hand, and the tree-decked acres of "leafy Warwickshire" on the other, seemed to obsess Cadbury. More than any other model employer and town-builder he determined to create a "city in a garden". In the late eighteen-nineties the outcome of the first phase of extensive development became apparent. Broad stretches of park, lakes and recreational grounds, and a wood preserved in its original outlines, covered almost as much land, in this early stage, as did the new houses themselves. The latter were well built, often in the style of Tudor cottages, with rough-cast and half-timbering on gables, to echo the indigenous oak-framed buildings of the county, some of which have been preserved, and resited, in Bournville. The house styles were not highly ornate, however, and although no one shape was ever repeated in uniform rows, there is a common scale and a common simplicity of treatment of surfaces and decorative detail that give both originality and unity to the town (if such it might be called). As Bournville progressed, two main styles of building dominated its architectural scene; one is that based on the timbered Tudor building with its sharply-angled gables and tall chimneys; the other derives from the small town-cottage of Georgian

Fig. 138. Houses in a green setting, Bournville

Fig. 139. Willow Road, Bournville

times where a simple façade with symmetrically placed windows had replaced the earlier medieval front (fig. 138).[4] Gardens, with a minimum of enclosure, and trees of great variety planted in the grass verges of almost every road, produce scenes like those in fig. 139 and help to create a type of town landscape which is peculiarly English, yet which has been all too rarely equalled in its consistency elsewhere in this country. At Bournville houses were built by Cadbury Brothers Ltd. and by Bournville Tenants Ltd. to designs by little-known architects. The process illustrates the new kind of partnership or community control of town-building taste.

W. H. Lever, the founder of Port Sunlight, and Joseph Rowntree who followed closely the lead of Bournville at New Earswick outside York, produced further good examples of the Romantic style in their model villages. In both places brick is used to good effect, as it is at Bournville, and with their picturesque grouping of buildings, and their careful use of green spaces and trees, these towns helped to spread the idea of the compatibility of town and country. The style of building common to these model settlements has continued to be favoured right down to the present time, not only in small private developments and council-estates, but even in some of the New Towns of the nineteen-fifties and sixties. Once a style has been adopted for a large comprehensive project, it is probably destined to make a very big contribution to the total townscape, and the championing of the rural village idea by the architects who carried out the plans of Ebenezer Howard (the founder of the Garden City Movement) helped to ensure the popularity of Romantic design in many towns at a later date.

Howard, like other reformers, was concerned with sociological questions and not with purely architectural ones. But while some of his predecessors had stopped short at housing experiments, and others had only been concerned to gear industrial villages to one particular industry, Howard tried to answer the basic question "What is a town?". This is not the place for a discussion of Howard's principles, but it is necessary to see that what is good about building at Letchworth and Welwyn Garden City—the successful products of the Garden City Movement—is owing not just to the merit of individual buildings, but even more to their part in a planned realisation of a town as a balanced community serving the fullest possible range of social and economic needs.

A town planned from the start to fulfil certain prescribed functions, built in a mere two decades—in contrast to the centuries which elapse while most towns emerge as recognisable forms—and yet intended to re-create the atmosphere of an ancient village, might seem like a recipe for artistic disaster. Yet in Letchworth, the first and the most successful Garden City, such disaster was averted. To-day the town's architecture fails to satisfy only in its public buildings and shopping-centre— where its designers abandoned the Romantic style for the prevailing fashion in Classical revivals, namely a kind of Georgian in which the detail is a fair imitation, but where the basic proportions and the chief formal elements of the buildings have not been subjected to that tireless scrutiny and reconsideration—at the "drawing-board" stage—without which the justification for a Classical design ceases to exist.

The first achievement of Letchworth is the pattern it makes on the ground. This pattern is a mixture of a few rigid geometric shapes and a majority of seemingly haphazard ones, some of the latter being directed in all probability by physical features and former boundaries or tracks which were elements of the agricultural land before the town came to be built. In spite of Lewis Mumford's reference to Raymond Unwin's "love for the rambling layout of medieval German hill towns", and the avoidance of "mechanical stereotypes" in the original Letchworth street-plan,[5] the first proposals are surprisingly formal (fig. 140). Fortunately perhaps, though not in opposition to Howard's own assumption that a Garden City could take on an indefinite number of shapes to suit the conditions of the site and the type of community occupying it, the present pattern of the town has lost most of the straight lines which were drawn by the designers Barry Parker and Raymond Unwin, and is difficult to distinguish from an overgrown English village except in its consistent lack of crowded or closely built-up quarters (fig. 141).

Fig. 140. The plan for Letchworth by Barry Parker and Raymond Unwin

At ground level the impressive thing about Letchworth is its cohesion. In spite of a variety of structural shapes, and the well-wooded character of its streets, there is no difficulty in recognising the aim of its builders. Although still small (it has a population of about 26,230) it has a distinctly urban air. Its styles are the styles of London's suburbia, but they have been made into a meaningful pattern. Key-points in the composition of Letchworth, like the Town Square and the approach to the railway station, are well shaped and have an appearance of dignity combined with an air of efficiency. It is true that the fine trees in streets like Broadway are as responsible for the town's good looks as are the buildings themselves—perhaps even more responsible—but they are a part of the plan (which envisaged the ultimate effect of matured trees in suitable settings) and, indeed, without them the conception of a "Garden City" would be meaningless. Trees, shrubs, gardens, grassy side-walks, greens and public parks are the garden city's equivalent of the stone court-yards and paved piazzas, the boulevards and flights of steps, the arches and sculpture in the Classical city.

Fig. 141. Letchworth today (O.S. $2\frac{1}{2}''$ to mile, 1956)

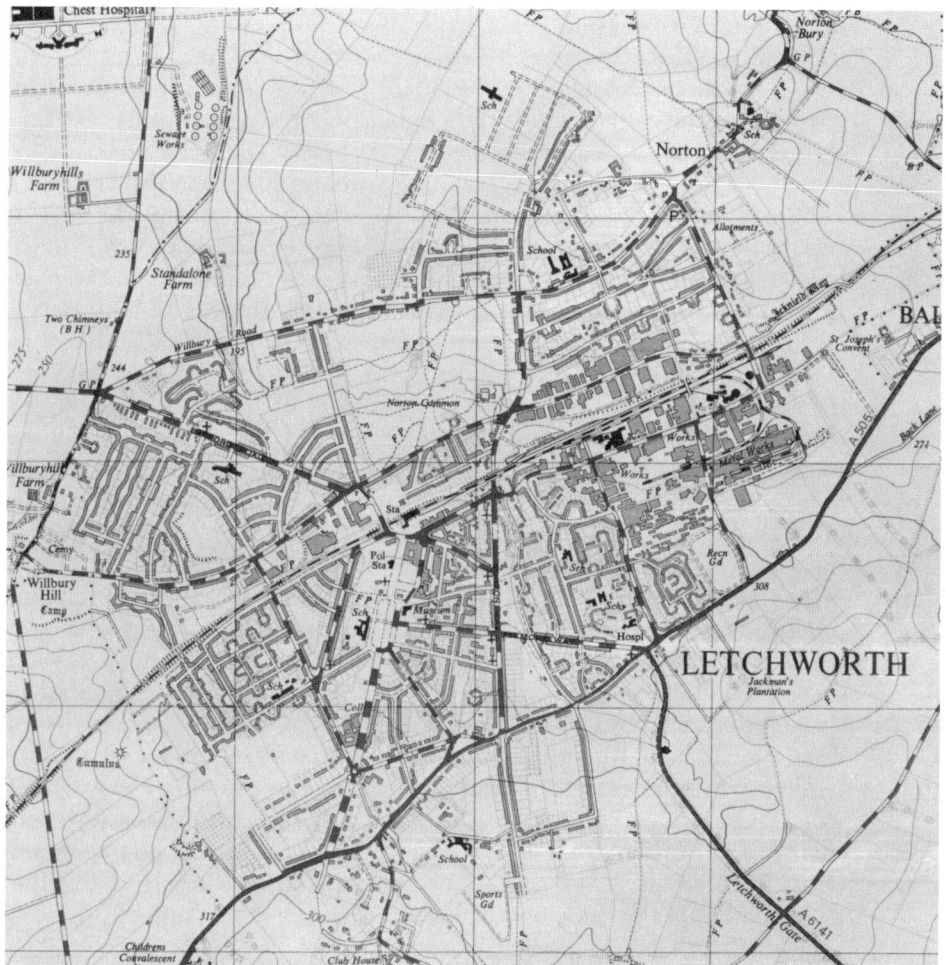

Built right to the edge of the commercial and industrial quarters of Letchworth, and yet very little disturbed by them, are the residential districts. Here the trees are even more impressive. A profuse variety has been planted and many of them are now reaching maturity. Instead of the inevitable flowering cherries and almond trees favoured to-day for street decoration, a mixture of deciduous and evergreen forest trees, with contrasting natural forms, has been chosen. Tall trees, "weeping" trees, trees with feathery leaves and trees with broad ones, big-boled trees and trees with slender trunks, stiff-looking trees and trees which sway in the breeze, all contribute to an animated but not restless scene in which houses play a secondary and unobtrusive role (fig. 142).

Just as houses had been architect-designed at Bournville and Port Sunlight, so they were at Letchworth. Here, in particular, the Garden City Company, and later the local authority, exerted a firm control over the siting and the type of buildings erected, and encouraged in various ways the employment of young architects to design cottage-style workers' houses of a type which is now familiar, but which in its day was a startling innovation. "The publicity that the scheme received drew the attention of London journalists who came to see what queer thing was arising in Hertfordshire. The houses were of a kind new to most people then . . . and the red roofs and white rough-cast walls, the green paint and waterbutts, were material for comic papers."[6]

The work of architects like Webb, Shaw, Parker and Unwin is less immediately impressive, less photogenic, too, than such town designing as is found, say, in eighteenth-century Edinburgh or in the early nineteenth-century estates of the West End of London, and it was unfortunate that, when town centres, municipal buildings, industrial offices and the like were built during the first decades of the twentieth century, no style was evolved (say in the Shaw tradition) which might have led to a harmonising of principal and lesser buildings in the new urban areas. Instead it was deemed proper in most cases to lean heavily on the styles of the past, probably because of the mystique surrounding anything derived from Classical canons. Certainly the first builders of twentieth-century town centres were guilty of the assumption that to give a weighty and aloof face to a building was to invest it with the necessary visual qualities to accompany its status if it were a council-office block, a library, a central shopping unit or even a railway station. Uncertainty, then, went hand in hand with the new forms of town-building. The great explosion of urban development following the First World War occurred at the same time as this stage of hesitancy in British architecture and town design. Out of the experiments, already described, in the use of medieval forms, new "clean" native lines might have emerged which would not have been out of step with developments in the use of entirely new materials for building, like steel and glass. Instead, "run down" Classicism and "watered down" Romanticism became all too frequently the standard shapes for the great phase of urban sprawl and main-road "ribbon" development which spread across the country after 1918, and which was unfortunately still not adequate in scale to lead to the overdue clearance of most of the worst slums which continued to survive in the inner zones of towns and cities. But some of the building that took place in the twenties and thirties is more creditable than the severest critics of this period will allow, and this, together with other development of the time, will be looked at in the next chapter

Fig. 142. Trees in the townscape of Letchworth

10. *Romantic Town Scenery*

continued

F. J. OSBORN estimated that between 1898 and 1944 the equivalent of three hundred towns could have been built from the formula of Ebenezer Howard, if the increase in building which actually took place during that period had been directed accordingly. "Yet", he says (referring to Letchworth and Welwyn), "we have only two garden cities, with a combined population of less than 40,000".[1] Since Osborn wrote, the New Towns of south-east England, and others in the North-East and in Scotland have given new life to Howard's principles and Unwin's plans. But the period from just before the First World War to the outbreak of the second, while it did see the spread of suburban growth of a type which often deserves, too well, the various titles which it has inspired (the current and perhaps the best being "subtopia"), is one of great interest, containing much forgotten achievement. Hampstead Garden Suburb, which has perhaps failed to receive the attention due to it, is a key to most of what is good in the period now under review. "Suburb" itself having become a term of abuse, and the social structure of the Hampstead example having failed to show the variety that its planners had hoped for, its brilliant designing, as an answer to the problem of housing "big-city" dwellers, has sometimes been overlooked. The Hampstead experiment got under way well before the First World War, and had attracted so much attention that, as Ashworth says, "By 1914, apart from Letchworth Garden City and early schemes such as Bournville and Port Sunlight, at least fifty-two schemes for garden suburbs were completed or in progress".[2] The continued growth of these projects and many more like them, together with the spread of other suburban development after 1918, means that the full impact of Hampstead Garden Suburb was made in the inter-war years.

The plan of roads, houses and open spaces on the north side of the famous Heath is illustrated in its original form in fig. 143. This was chiefly the work of Raymond Unwin, and building itself proceeded in the main by means of the formation of co-partnership societies.[3] The character of the plan is unreservedly Romantic, apart from the formality of Central Square, chiefly designed by Edwin Lutyens. Even this, in spite of some Classical details, has more of the Tudor courtyard or quadrangle in it than of the piazza or forum, and is an almost wholly successful attempt to re-create a late medieval atmosphere (fig. 144). The happiest designs are the

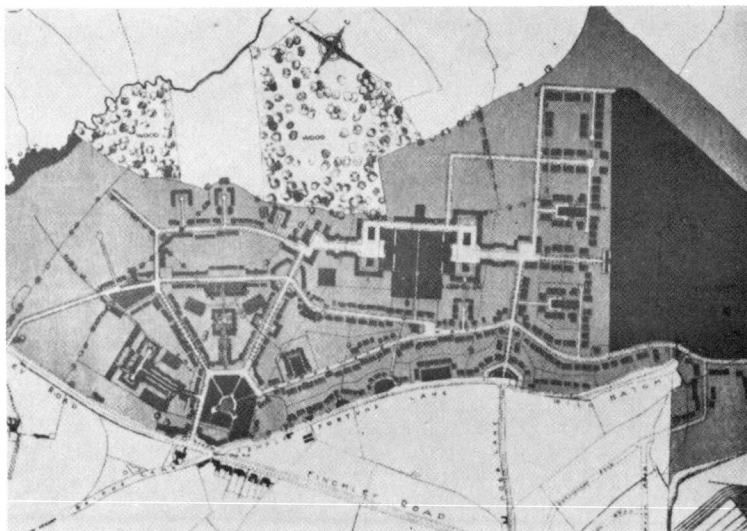

Fig. 143. The original plan in 1905 of Hampstead Garden Suburb

Fig. 144. Part of Central Square, Hampstead Garden Suburb

Fig. 145. Houses in Temple Fortune Hill, Hampstead Garden Suburb

house-groups in such streets as Erskine Hill and Temple Fortune Hill (figs. 145 and 146). The architect-planner who seeks to create a Romantic townscape must, by the very nature of the task he has set himself, design unobtrusively, and with the appearance of casual informality. Consequently his results at their best are undramatic and have an appearance of inevitability about them. The great achievement of Hampstead Garden Suburb is that its residential building really has got most of the things that we admire in the domestic architecture of the Middle Ages, and now that time has matured the sites and building materials, it fully realises the aim of its promoters, expressed in the following extract from a statement of aims by Hampstead Tenants Ltd. in 1905:

> "We aim at preserving natural beauty. Our object is so to lay out the ground that every tree may be kept, hedgerows duly considered, and the foreground of the distant view preserved, if not as open fields, yet as a gardened district, the buildings kept in harmony with the surroundings."[4]

Note too the artistic aspects of the scheme in its original broad outline, referred to by its founder Henrietta Barnett:

> ". . . the cottages and houses should be limited on an average to eight to an acre; the roads should be forty feet wide and the houses should be at least fifty feet apart, gardens occupying the intervening space; . . . the plot divisions should not be walls, but hedges or trellis or wire fences; . . . every road should be lined with trees . . . making where possible a colour scheme with the hedges . . . the houses should be so planned that none should spoil each other's outlook or rob its neighbour of beauty."[5]

Fig. 146. Houses in Erskine Hill, Hampstead Garden Suburb

Fig. 147. Early twentieth-century housing in Leicester

The skill required to carry out such an intention successfully must not be under-rated. The failure of most inter-war building to match up to Hampstead is not just a matter of economics. It is far more difficult to reach a moderate standard of good taste with the varied materials and shapes available to the builder of Romantic scenes than it is to achieve modest success with construction which embodies the symmetry and regularity of Classicism. Had the period of maximum territorial expansion of our towns coincided with the peak of Classical taste, the English countryside would have disappeared beneath monotonous rows of houses of identical shape and dimension, and endless straight streets which ignored the curves of our rounded hills or the twists of meandering valleys and ancient tracks. We have fared no worse to have inherited, instead, the acres of estates, municipal and private, which now so indelibly mark the outskirts of our towns and cities.

Striking proof of the effect of suburban building, both by local authorities and private building firms, is given by large-scale plans and aerial photographs illustrating the period in question. The East Midlands, where the economic depression of the thirties struck less hard than it did in areas of specialisation in heavy industry, shows the uncompromising patterns which were made on the landscape at this time. Figs. 147 and 148 are air photographs comparing conditions in Leicester, derived from the late nineteenth and early twentieth century, with those from the period just before the outbreak of the Second World War, and the map (fig. 149) illustrates the two zones represented by these periods.

Fig. 148. Aerial view of the
Braunstone area of Leicester

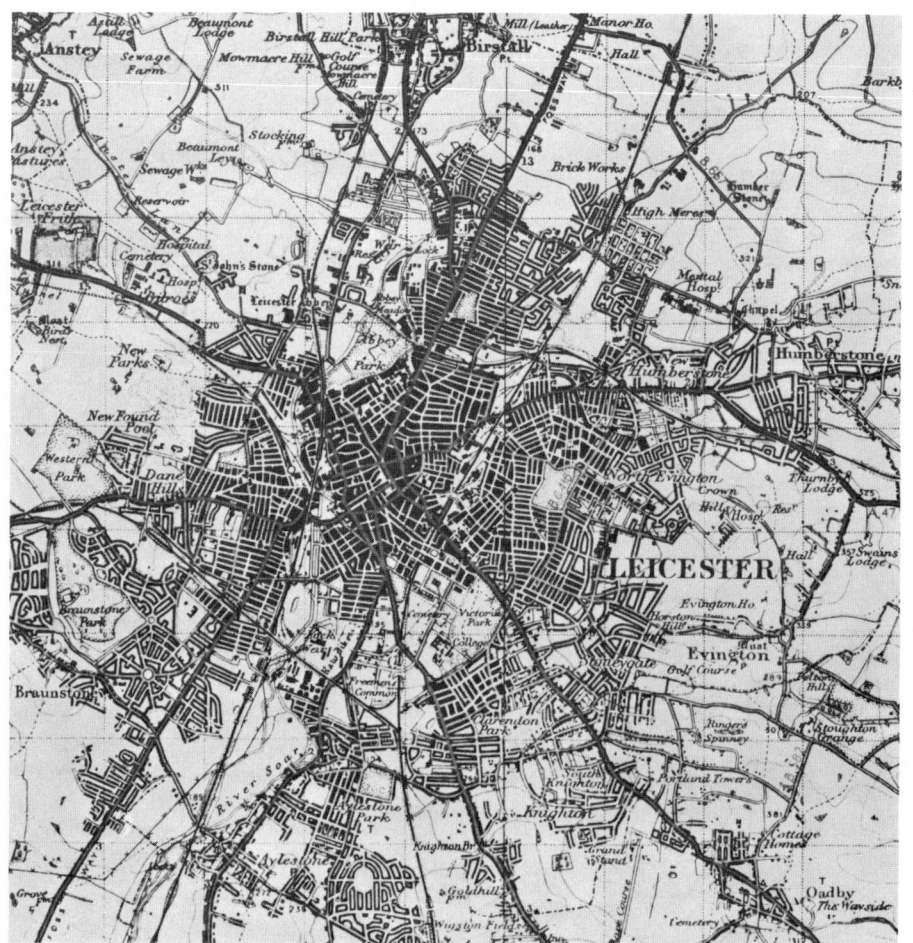

Fig. 149.
The O.S. 1″ to the mile
map of Leicester
showing conditions
in approximately 1939.
Braunstone is on the
west side of the city

The city of Leicester is one where the tradition of well-spread-out building dates from the beginnings of industrialism. W. G. Hoskins has pointed out that, unlike its neighbour Nottingham, Leicester was successful in enclosing its open fields at an early date, and never had to face the problems of building high-density working-class housing on limited space in its central districts.[6] Nineteenth-century Leicester was a dramatic example of terrace-house building around a medieval core, and the inter-war map of the city (fig. 149) can be read like three condensed chapters of history describing the irregular nucleus, the ribbed intermediate zone, and the loose net of suburban extensions. The third of these "chapters" displays the Romantic townscape, in plan form, as it was conceived by local authority architects and the designers of private housing-estates. The well-balanced map-pattern of roads and houses to the west of the city around Braunstone Park is an excellent example of municipal housing development; the random snippets of suburban network, on a similar scale, on the east side around Stoneygate illustrate the residential projects resulting from private enterprise, and a special point of interest is Humberstone Garden City—a minute survival of the movement from which it takes its name—which has petered out and got lost in the mass of other suburban development.

Braunstone was, in the early years of the present century, a village separated from the western limits of Leicester by an estate with a mansion, meadows, a park and a lake. In the years following 1918, the owner of this estate, Major R. N. Winstanley, was subjected to the inevitable pressure which the demand for building land was applying to landowners all around the city. He eventually sold out to Leicester Corporation, in preference to the alternative of giving way to private speculators, because, "If his beloved Braunstone must be sacrificed, and it was clear that eventually it must, better far that it should be turned into a pleasant garden suburb than that the speculative builders should chop it up, and lay it out on a purely commercial basis".[7] By 1930 thousands of houses had been built at Braunstone, and thousands more were to come. A contemporary judgment informs us that the city corporation "had not done all that was asked of it, but it had not done badly" and "more progress has been made in the ten years it [the corporation] has been setting the fashion in cottage building, than in a couple of generations of pre-war domestic building".[8] To-day, when society is preoccupied with yet further plans for extending and rebuilding its towns, it is instructive to take a close look at a place like Braunstone as a representative example of a somewhat forgotten and often despised period of urban development.

The new Braunstone has been built on very gently rolling country and surrounds a splendid public park formed from the old estate. Although the suburb is built on the assumption that low-density housing forms part of some inviolable principle, and although the impression made by the air photograph (fig. 148) is of buildings of monotonously low-level construction scattered in a too-regularly dispersed pattern, the details of site and of individual house-designs make the ground-level views interesting at every turn, and the place achieves a feeling of neighbourliness often lost in such extensive schemes as this one. At the same time there is usually room for garages to be added to houses not originally designed for the car

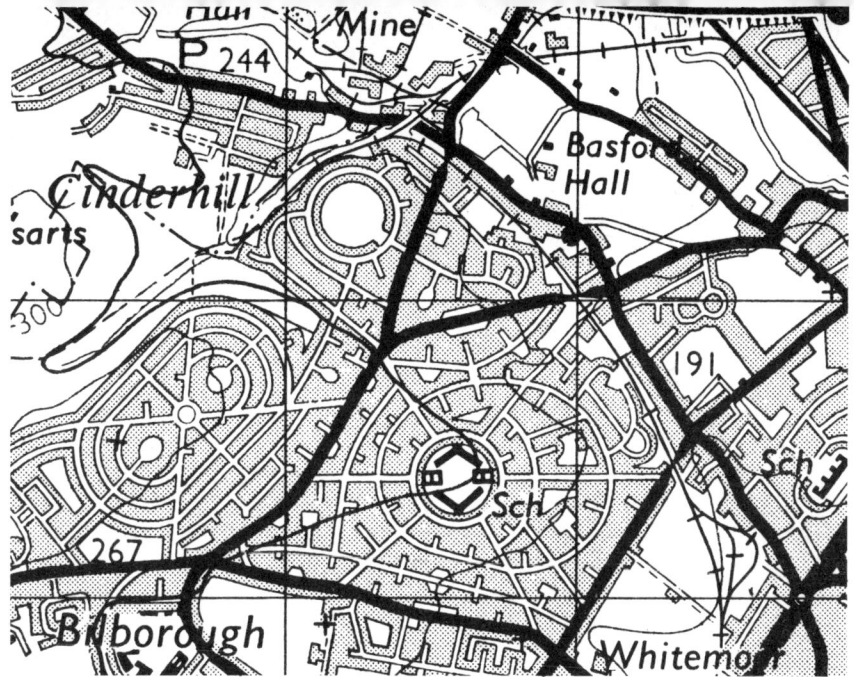

Fig. 150. Plan of housing estates, Bilborough, Nottingham, enlarged from O.S. 1" to the mile, sheet 112, New Popular Edition

age, or at least for groups of garages to be placed at the end of rows, or on other spare land. The road plan is an interesting example of the tendency of this period to "Romanticise" a Vitruvian pattern. Almost all idea of symmetry has disappeared: the planner seems to have started with some intention of using concentric circles and squares and then to have distorted these into sinuous arabesque lines or irregular patterns of rectilinear forms (fig. 149). Compared, for example, with the much more formal layout at Bilborough near Nottingham, twenty miles to the north (fig. 150), Braunstone is a good attempt at producing, from drawing-board inventions, some relief from the cruel repetitiveness of the nineteenth-century streets, while avoiding the late Classical solution of rigid squares and circles. The Braunstone type of road-network is found in estates—particularly those built by local authorities—in all parts of the country. Such networks are often very imaginative, but they show one great limitation; through obsessive concern with the need to avoid crowding at all costs, the plans never allow for concentration to occur—as it might have done at certain natural focal points—nor do they permit the minor open spaces like roundabouts, widened grass verges at street corners and the like, to extend occasionally into irregular shapes which would make them seem less like little preserves of the municipal landscape gardener. Town plan patterns like those at Braunstone must surely owe something to the earlier movement in art known as "Art Nouveau", and they remind us that the architect making fashionable shapes on his drawing-board is still a major partner of the engineer and the social reformer in deciding on the forms of our cities.

But—to return to the Leicester suburb—the appearance of the winding main roads, and of the varied side streets and cul-de-sacs is, to-day, pleasing and harmonious. The trees are reaching maturity: schools, shops and churches—some of them very new—are making the urban scene more varied, and, although the mobile shop is still an important part of everyday life, there is a rooted look about Braunstone that must surprise anyone who only knew it in its early days. This effect is partly achieved by the fact that the house-designs rely heavily on traditional shapes, and many of them have a Georgian appearance with overtones of the industrial cottage, but they also include such features as gables and fairly steep roofs of more Romantic character. Perhaps the most impressive thing about the planning of Braunstone, when seen at close quarters, is the way in which the variety of the individual designs of the houses is never allowed to destroy the general simplicity of the cottage-style building. Included amongst the materials of construction are tiles of several different colours, slate, rough-cast, and a number of bricks of pleasing quality. Constant variation in the building-line makes the street-picture from ground level of yet further interest, but it is unfortunate that most houses are rather box-like in their proportions, and that they are almost invariably semi-detached. Occasionally interesting groupings like that of fig. 151 show what can be done in the direction of more imaginative arrangement.

Fig. 151. Housing at Braunstone, Leicester

Fig. 152. Welwyn Garden City from the air, showing the mixing of formal and informal planning

Fig. 153. Recent housing at Welwyn

The Braunstone estate has not been chosen for its exceptional qualities, as was the case with examples like Bournville and Letchworth. It is one of a large number of such suburban areas developed by local authorities in the inter-war years and it shows that these places are surviving much of the criticism that has been levelled against them. It would be well if thought and money were to be spared to repair some of the deficiencies of these areas—such as the lack of social amenities for most age-groups, except the "under tens", and the scarcity of architectural focal points and landmarks—and yet to maintain and enhance their many undoubted attractions, such as their peacefulness and healthiness, their freedom from traffic congestion and street-sign clutter, their greenness and their success in preserving considerable individuality of architectural character within a planned, community-owned townscape.

*   *   *   *   *

The second Garden City to be built according to the principles of Ebenezer Howard was at Welwyn. The character of this town, which was begun soon after the First World War, owes much to the primary aim of its planners to establish, beyond the limits of the London commuter belt, a self-contained community of workpeople and professional classes. As does that of its county neighbour Letchworth, the town-pattern of Welwyn includes clearly-defined zones for industry, residence, shopping, recreation and so on, and here, too, the insistence on greensward and trees as an intimate accompaniment to all phases of the town's design is a result of the most conscientious adherence to the belief that a living-space can be created that is at once both town and country. But Welwyn seems more dispersed than Letchworth, and the density of the central area is very low. There is much less of an urban "feeling" about the place, and it may be that here enthusiasm for the Garden City idea has overreached itself, and what has resulted is, in fact, neither country nor town.

So well scattered are the blocks and individual buildings of the town centre of Welwyn Garden City that it is difficult to detect, from ground level, that the plan of the streets is in fact Vitruvian. This characteristic of the layout, together with the neo-Georgian character of most of the shops and public buildings, shows a surprisingly strong leaning towards the Classical in what, in respect of its setting, is a Romantic town. The same confusion of thought exists in the design of houses and streets. The latter, unlike the main thoroughfares, are generally curved, or at least are arranged in a variety of fairly informal patterns; the placing of houses, too, is sometimes consciously irregular (fig. 152). But the style of the houses themselves is based on the Georgian cottage, and even very recent development has retained this characteristic (fig. 153). Individual houses are almost exclusively in brick and tile, and have the rather heavy wooden trimming and thick glazing bars which have characterised most twentieth-century imitations of Georgian windows.

In large towns the first half of the twentieth century has, perhaps, seen something even more striking than the addition of a wide belt of suburban estates to the former built-up areas. The main roads that lead into, and out of, the city centres have undergone very complex changes under the combined influence of commerce and motor transport. Constant changes in the pace of economic development, and the mainly steady rise in the value of land along the chief arteries of town traffic, have led to a long, restless phase of tearing down and building up which no planning legislation has, as yet, managed to stop.

A journey northwards along London's Finchley Road, by way of the Great North Road to the edge of the Green Belt at High Barnet, illustrates the extent to which styles have proliferated without any relationship to each other. At the junction of roads at Swiss Cottage, at the southern end of Finchley Road, an absolute riot of materials and styles jostle for the road frontage; white tiles (of the London Underground); imitation Swiss chalet "architecture"; a huge mock-Tudor shop-group; concrete, in modern blocks of flats; the brick and Portland stone of mock-Georgian (also in flats)—these overpower the remains of Victorian stucco and the red brick of Edwardian Baroque. Compared with the junction, the beginning of the Finchley Road itself is more consistent, and is made from red brick, with tall shop-terraces capped by Dutch gables, followed by other terraces of large houses and flats. The propagation of styles continues, but brick predominates amongst the materials; skyline levels drop after Parsifal Road is passed; then there appear substantial houses, detached and semi-detached, and mostly of mock-Tudor type. At the junction with Hendon Way, rough-cast makes its appearance, and so does half-timbering, heralding (soon after a pleasant little crop of mid-Victorian or earlier houses) the most common type of semi-detached dwellings to be found in city suburbs, with their bay windows, steep gables and mixtures of brick, rough-cast and timber. Shrubs and green plots in gardens, and occasional trees, are beginning to be noticeable, and glimpses down the side roads give impressions of extensive development on suburban lines. At the cross-roads, near Golders Green Underground Station, is another outbreak of mixed styles on the fronts of tall buildings: "Branch-Bank Greek", "Picture-Palace Italianate" and "Shopping-Block Dutch-Classical" are the sort of hybrid titles that spring to mind (fig. 154). As the Finchley Road continues northwards, more "semi-d's" appear, some built almost entirely of a dark brownish-grey brick and not at all bad looking; then a very bad mock-Georgian row of shops crowds the roadside. As the North Circular Road is reached, building becomes more scattered, and beyond some green spaces and trees are seen tiers of flats, some in "Early Modern Movement style" and some in neo-Classical mode. In Regent's Park Road is a long "terrace" of closely-packed pairs of houses, probably of the early years of the present century, and then come more modern flats, this time with walls of brick, glass and concrete, in total contrast to semi-detached "Tudors" with half-timbered gables. Some good nineteenth-century villas and a pleasing terrace intervene before a stretch of mock "Queen Anne" and red-brick "Norman Shaw" types of building. (Behind all this are obviously vast suburbs of small villas, detached and semi-detached.) Near Tally-ho Corner, low Victorian bay-windowed houses—some of them Italianate—are well set back from the road, with good garden greenery, and at the Corner itself, in spite of a lot of alteration

Fig. 154. Part of the Finchley Road, near Golders Green

and the brutality of some "modernistic" shop-fronts, the line of the Victorian building still "gets through".

Now the general building level gets lower and the units are a little less tightly knit. But the contrasts in style and scale can still be dramatic. Cinemas stand out with their peculiar adaptations of forms from the palaces and temples of a range of real and imaginary ancient civilisations, mostly of the Middle East variety, and—a pleasing foil to the confusion of much of the building hereabouts—some good modern flats of modest scale with well-balanced areas of concrete and glass make an appearance. At the county boundary only the trees lining the road are pleasant to look upon, and "by-pass variegated" houses dot the landscape. Red-tiled roofs seem to be everywhere, and pebble-dash and half-timbering stretch away in all directions. The rolling relief of the one-time countryside is pleasant enough, and there is much scattering of trees amongst the rust-coloured roofs. The air is clean, and these final acres of Greater London will continue to seem tolerable until (if the Green Belt yields) another twenty years of sprawl have left them too far from the fields to breathe, any longer, the freshness of Hertfordshire. The Great North Road continues through Barnet, where occasional Georgian and early Victorian house-fronts have escaped ruin, and the flint church is almost the first building of note since the West End. The general hotch-potch of styles is quite pleasing in High Street, and, on the very threshold of real country, some well-designed modern houses and bungalows, amongst fine Georgian neighbours, prompt the hope that the next few decades will produce something better than the last six.

Looking back along this artery through twentieth-century London, it is difficult to see the scenery that has been created as a part of any tradition, and only by the most flexible exercising of the imagination can the Finchley Road be described as part of a Romantic townscape. What has happened to the notion that the studied arrangement of revived medieval shapes can be made to produce a Romantic semi-rural picture, is that it was never expanded to apply to any aspects of town-growth other than small, self-contained residential units. Main-road development in particular has been left to chance, and in the end is neither Classical nor Romantic, nor even a good mixture of both, but a no-man's-land of tastelessness which it will take, at the present rate of the growth of a design-sense amongst our public leaders, at least a century to replace.

But for all the criticisms of philistinism that have been levelled against it, the present age is remarkable for an ability—admittedly rare—to look at its artistic heritage in town design and to take some steps to preserve the best of it. This, as we have seen, is being done in some of the John Nash areas of London. It is also sometimes thought that circumstances might warrant the designing of something appropriate in scale and shape for the rest of the urban environment in which such new construction is to take place. This kind of concern for environment (some might call it sentimentality) rarely if ever existed in former centuries, when, it seems, once a new style of building had been introduced there was little hesitation in preferring it to everything else. The Romantic townscape may be far from the thoughts of most architects and planners at the present time, but if its characteristics, of informality and irregularity, seem appropriate to a project, it may sometimes be found claiming

Fig. 155. Cottages by
Basil Spence, Dunbar

Fig. 156.
The housing
scheme by
Basil Spence
in Dunbar

the interest of designers whose normal style is suited to something totally different. An example of this is to be found in an out-of-the-way corner of Scotland, in the little seaside town of Dunbar, where Basil Spence has shown, in planning a scheme of cottages to fill a derelict area near the old harbour, how, with simple means and traditional shapes, a little group of houses can be built to look as if they had always been there (figs. 155 and 156). Only a Romantic feeling for towns could have made the Dunbar idea into a reality. As we see some of our architects tentatively exploring a few medieval shapes once again (there is a modern echo of half-timber patterns in a new building at Stratford-on-Avon, for example, and several attempts to use a fretted roof-line, reminiscent of gables, can be seen in our cities), it may not be too much to hope that the next phase of the Romantic townscape is on its way.

Fig. 157. The Forth Rail Bridge

Fig. 158. The Crystal Palace
as originally designed by Joseph Paxton

11. *The Modern Town*

A SHAPE like that of the Forth Railway Bridge (built in the years from 1882 to 1889 (fig. 157)) was so different from anything that architects were accustomed to produce in the nineteenth century that it was a very long time before it was appreciated that designs representing a solution to engineering problems were helping to cause a revolution in more conventional fields of construction. To-day, when the majority of major buildings arise around a framework of steel or of reinforced concrete, and when curtain walls of glass often leave revealed an inner structure demonstrating its own functional attractions, it is easy enough to see how much modern town-design owes to the early builders of bridges, railway stations, market halls and the like, and to such a remarkable creation as the Crystal Palace designed by Joseph Paxton for the Great Exhibition of 1851 (fig. 158). But, partly because Britain was slow to learn the lessons which were first taught in her own towns, the process whereby the work of the early designers for the machine age was transformed into a building style for our own cities (a style that is now international) is not easily traced. Nikolaus Pevsner has shown that it was through the daring advocacy of a few American and European architects, and especially through the offices of Walter Gropius and a group of artists and craftsmen at the Weimar Bauhaus, that "the new (architectural) style, the genuine and legitimate style of our century, was achieved by 1914".[1] This style is well illustrated by the model factory of Gropius and Meyer exhibited at the Werkbund Exhibition in 1914 (fig. 159).

It is not necessary to be concerned in detail here with the ways in which the Arts and Crafts Movement in Britain, the post-Impressionist phase of painting in France, and the short-lived episode of Art Nouveau helped in their different ways to start a tradition that was as opposed to the medievalism of the Garden City builders as it was to the academism of the still active Classicists. These movements left only slight traces on the British scene, though there did appear, as a scattered phenomenon throughout the nineteen-twenties and the nineteen-thirties, a kind of building which was a direct successor to the works of Continental and American architects. If they are found on prominent sites these isolated elements in our townscapes wield an influence out of proportion to their size. It was characteristic of cinemas and garages that they took on shapes ostensibly in the "modern manner", though this was usually degraded to a point of mediocrity (at best) and, by the nature of the functions carried on within them, these two types of places force themselves into prominence in the urban scene. One or two firms, which consistently

Fig. 159.
Model Factory
by Gropius & Meyer,
1914

Fig. 160. Houses at Stanmore, Middlesex

Fig. 161. The buildings of Quarry Hill, Leeds

adopted modern styles in the inter-war years, also built in conspicuous places and frequently altered the appearance of towns by taking over important corner sites and clothing them with such surfaces as shining black marble, inset with green neon tube-lighting. Some flats and private villas were built in what might be called "Bauhaus style", with ruthlessly plain surfaces, flat roofs and large, steel-framed windows, but very few areas of small domestic buildings were constructed in this manner, and it was only sporadically adopted by private or council-house estates in a consistent overall design (fig. 160). There were some noteworthy exceptions to this latter generalisation towards the end of the inter-war period, including the famous flats at Quarry Hill in Leeds, which not only represent a piece of town planning of importance in the history of the rehousing of the occupants of working-class slums, but are also an experiment which helped to set the fashion in high blocks, surrounded by open spaces, for future generations of designers of high-density areas near city centres.

Quarry Hill, planned to house 3,250 people on twenty-six acres, was begun in 1935. The original scheme included 938 flats and twenty shops, and had 82 per cent of its area devoted to open space. There are a community hall, a nursery school, seven children's playgrounds for various ages, and adults' sports facilities. This catalogue gives some idea of the range of needs that the scheme was intended to satisfy, and the aerial photograph (fig. 161) shows the kind of arrangements made by the groups of buildings. From ground level the buildings of Quarry Hill are markedly bold in design and demonstrate well the features derived from the early modern architects—that is, a form is presented which is directly related to the sub-structure, while a few clearly-defined areas of contrasting materials serve, in the most restrained sense, to underline, decoratively, the broad lines and masses of the structure. Very recently the Quarry Hill buildings have been completely redecorated and in the course of this "face-lift" the original bands of brickwork have been obliterated by what looks like cement wash, leading to an even more severe façade than was originally intended. The overhaul of the flats does, however, make possible, nearly thirty years after their construction, a realistic assessment of Quarry Hill as a contribution to townscape. This assessment—the view of the present writer—is that the pre-war Leeds housing scheme is a bold, even a brilliant, failure. Built before techniques which give to large masses a feeling of lightness had been widely adopted, it now seems heavy and clumsy. The long, curving repetitive façades, reminiscent of medieval castle walls (but without the variety of shape which these usually possess) mean that little thought has had to be given to the proportions of the buildings, and from ground level there is no one point from which the mass seems intended to be viewed. At the same time there is not the compensation that exists, in much of our more recent building, of elongated or soaring repeat-patterns of ribs, panels and the like, which, especially when seen from positions near the base of buildings, are enlivening and uplifting visual experiences. Worse than this, many of the open spaces which were intended, presumably, as areas not only for bodily relaxation but also for visual contrast to the severe forms of the architecture, become patches of mud in wet weather, and patches of bare earth when it is dry. The smaller open spaces are clearly of the wrong type, both from the practical and aesthetic point of view, and should be paved or cobbled to give a fully man-made appearance to a type of town-building that can never hope to have the qualities of a garden suburb.

Quarry Hill is an early example of a kind of townscape that is still making headway in many of our cities and some of our larger towns. The clearance of areas of slum property, and of so-called "outworn" commercial buildings, and the replacement of these by tall blocks with comparatively small spaces around them, are short-sighted and haphazard ways of dealing with the business of building new towns within the old—which is the doubly-difficult problem set to the architects and planners of the second half of the twentieth century. Office-block building in London comes into this category of urban shapes, which are the result of the random growth of towers in little oases, and so do many working-class housing schemes, illustrated by the photograph of recent flats at Leeds (fig. 162).

Whatever the inadequacies, as pieces of town planning, of the foregoing examples, the completeness of the contrast between them and the features of the Romantic townscape is inescapable. They are, in any case, comparatively isolated phenomena, and it is necessary to turn elsewhere for illustrations of more comprehensive and more successful realisations, in town design, of the new sense of arrangements of space. But first we must look briefly at the causes of the new look that was being given to architecture during the early years of this century.

A most important step forward in helping to establish a new set of standards for architecture came with the appearance in 1917 of the magazine *De Stijl*, produced by a group of Dutch artists. This group included the painter Mondrian, and it is through a study of his work that we perhaps get nearest to the aesthetic ideas which underlie the modern movement in our own country. Mondrian represents a complete reversal of the trend of the nineteenth century towards Romanticism in art, and directs attention once more towards ancient Greece and Rome. If the Greeks

Fig. 162. Suburban development, Leeds

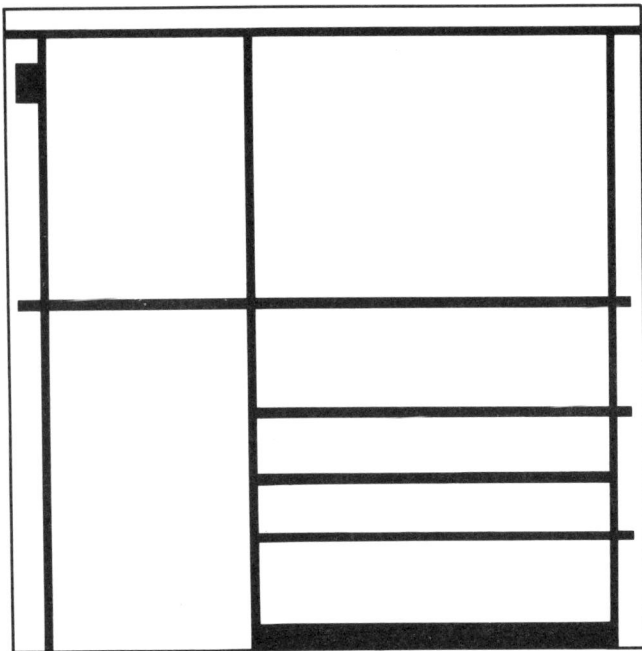

Fig. 163.
Sketch from a composition
by Mondrian, 1936

could arrive at a Golden Mean—which, in architectural terms was, in their view, the most completely satisfying relationship between two sides of a rectangle—and apply it to the building of temples and other great public buildings, then, Mondrian's works seem to say, any further complication of the rectangle, however simple, will enlarge the problem of maintaining a perfectly successful composition, and the results of solving this problem will be applicable to wider areas than those encompassed by one building or a part of a building. A study in lines and areas, like the one illustrated in fig. 163, is not a painting as the word was once understood, but an exercise in the development of the instinctive sense of the balance of forms. A line drawn parallel, and near to, one side of the rectangle or square can be balanced by another on the opposite side. Another line, also drawn across the space but at right-angles to the first two and somewhat away from the central position, makes the completion of balance in the whole composition an increasingly subtle problem. Mondrian solves it, in this case, with three horizontal lines and one broad band of similar length (coloured red in the original and therefore less "weighty" than it appears here) in the lower right-hand section of the picture plane, and a small black square (in the top left-hand corner) which, in spite of its size, by its shape and position draws the eye towards it, and gives it sufficient strength to resolve the rest of the lines and spaces into a completely satisfying composition. The longer one studies these arrangements of basic forms by Mondrian, the more compelling they become, until we finally recognise them as the bare bones that underlie almost all good modern design. "Mondrian", says Frederick Gore, "has influenced the architect and designer in every field of applied art, and has above all other painters left his mark upon our age".[2] This is certainly true of the applied art of the urban designer, who, not only in individual buildings but also in the grouping of buildings in space and in their arrangement in a ground-plan has, often unconsciously, followed the Dutch artist. In an individual building like the Research Building, Illinois Institute of Technology, by van der Rohe (fig. 164) the application of Mondrian is obvious. But a town plan can also have the same sort of characteristics as may be seen in a part of Harlow New Town, illustrated in fig. 165.

Fig. 164. Research building, Illinois, by Van der Rohe

Gore says, also, that it was Mondrian who "took painting back to the beginning again".[3] He also helped to take architecture back to the beginnings of European building and particularly to the assumptions underlying Greek architecture. The New Architecture of the twentieth century is thus a Classical movement, but in no sense a revival. Most conspicuously lacking are both the trappings of the Classical "orders", which a good deal of post-Renaissance design had mistaken for the really important formal qualities of ancient architecture, and the symmetrical arrangements of forms which have also been, too often, a substitute for really effective studies in proportion.

Fig. 165. Part of Harlow New Town, from the air

Fig. 166. A view of Kensal House, Ladbroke Grove, London

To appreciate the new Classicism, then, we must be prepared to search for qualities that may seem very new but are in fact very old. The grouping of the plain surfaces of buildings in the small towns of the coasts of the Mediterranean has, through instinct, and no doubt through a long association with the refinements of major Classical architecture, produced the sort of balance that was achieved by Mondrian on a two-dimensional surface, and this same kind of arrangement of shapes can be seen in unselfconscious groups of farm-buildings, of the eighteenth and early nineteenth century, in many parts of Britain. The designing of new towns, and of new centres to old towns, which is now a necessary social and economic act, is a test of the instincts of architects for that balancing of masses which should be the logical outcome of the Mondrian principles as they apply to the three dimensions of urban design.

Although they were very much the exception, some fine examples of designing in the "legitimate" style (as Pevsner puts it) were applied to building schemes in Britain before 1939, for instance the housing scheme in Ladbroke Grove, designed by E. Maxwell Fry. The illustration (fig. 166) is of a part of the design of this scheme —called Kensal House—which is, in fact, a series of units forming gently-curved terraces of flats, a nursery school and various other buildings. These were all com-

168

pleted by 1936. Seen now, after nearly thirty years of use, two things are especially striking about this intelligently-conceived work; the first is the failure of cement-washed concrete as a material for large, permanent surfaces; and the second, the very reasonable scale of the five-storied blocks, which are only a little higher than the neighbouring nineteenth-century terraces and which, by contemporary standards, seem to possess a friendly arrangement and scale. The very well-disposed balconies and windows, columns, entrances and canopies are much superior to the mass-produced fronts of most modern blocks, and it is sad that the quality of this design is being lost as surfaces deteriorate, and as the curving nursery school disappears beneath netting and barbed wire—presumably installed to prevent the children from climbing from the low flat roof into the gas-works next door.

It is chiefly in the post-war period, and especially in the building of New Towns, that the finest examples of modern town design are to be found. Since the town of Stevenage and its neighbourhood was designated a site for the building of a New Town—the first to be built as a result of the 1946 New Towns Act—the growth of its central area has attracted great attention and won well-deserved fame. It was not until 1959 that the shopping-centre was in full use, and it is now one of the largest of such areas in the country to be constructed entirely on the principle of the separation of pedestrians and traffic. A consciousness of the necessity for planning for the needs of a whole community—which has flavoured all town planning ideas in this country since the days of Ebenezer Howard—has, together with its contribution to traffic engineering, influenced the layout, scale and skyline of the Stevenage centre. The dance-hall, bowling-alley, pub and restaurant are as prominent in the scheme of buildings as are the canopied shop-fronts, the open market-stalls and the large stores. Even the offices of the Development Corporation—which maintain the traditional role of such places as prominent architectural features—are considered as part of a necessary and useful scheme. Although it is the tallest building in the area, it is set at a distant corner of Town Square, and not in a position of centralised splendour; it appears to watch with welcoming and friendly eyes the town over which—it would seem—it has a benevolent control.

The Stevenage town centre is the result of a revolution in our thinking about society's responsibility for the controlled development of urban life: at the height of success, the movement for town planning along community lines succeeded, at Stevenage, in recognising one more vital need of all civilised communities—beautiful surroundings. The townscape of the central area of Stevenage represents a new Renaissance in urban design: going back to fundamentals of aesthetics through Mondrian, its architects recaptured a purity of line and mass that is truly Classical, and this has proved entirely compatible with, and indeed necessary to, the realisation of the aims of sociological thinking of an equally fundamental kind. It is to be hoped that the success of good design in Stevenage will not be short-lived. There is a dangerous tendency for aesthetics to be given an apologetic last place in the list of advantages and achievements of a well-organised and efficient piece of town planning. But—as has often been shown—from early Greek art to the engineering works of the last century, efficiency and beauty are not only compatible, they can be inseparable.

Examples from Town Square, Stevenage, may be quoted to give substance to
this assessment of its place of importance in the development of British townscape.
The illustrations (figs. 167 and 168) are, like all consciously selected views of this
type, chosen to show off certain good features, and thus they make the already good
planning appear even better, with the aid of carefully composed photography. But
Town Square abounds in good views, and the problem for the illustrator of its
formal merits is how to convey the extensiveness of the patterns made by the well-
composed façades, and the successfulness of the flow of the sculptural shapes, rather
than how to find the one and only angle from which a single building of outstanding
merit may be seen (the problem of the photographer of historic townscapes in most
of our ancient cities). Standing in Town Square, Stevenage, is like being inside a
piece of sculpture which has been designed primarily for enjoyment from within.
The place invites exploration, and justifies the Development Corporation's assertion
that "Stevenage endeavours to create an intimate urban atmosphere reminiscent of
some of the older cathedral cities but without their disadvantages . . .".[4] This is by
no means an extravagant claim (and is certainly less so than that of many of our
ancient cities, when advertising themselves as "historic" while busily destroying
their heritage behind the mask of "urban redevelopment").

One final observation might be made, before ending this brief look at Stevenage,
concerning the use of trees in the urban setting. In most London squares, trees were
originally planted in rows, or other formal arrangements, and although the
maturity of these trees has brought with it soft outlines which contrast most pleasingly with the lines of the surrounding buildings, there is always a feeling of nature
being used to create architectural shapes, as was done with much greater rigidity in
the Italian gardens of the Renaissance. The present fashion—evident in Stevenage
—for involving the best groups and individual specimens of trees that have been
found on the original site, as a focus for a precinct, or as foreground or backdrop for
important buildings, is derived from the Garden City Movement. In other words,
the tree-groups, retained in their natural or semi-natural arrangements, are
Romantic elements in a Classical setting of buildings. This method of composition
can be most effective and is certainly a thoroughly British compromise; it should
not, however, be allowed to dominate all notions of how to embellish town architecture. There is a point where a tree, retained at all costs, its base encased in
cobble-sets or precinct paving, is an anachronism, while there is danger that sculpture—an art which has been given only scanty opportunities in our new townscapes
—will be forgotten.

Other New Towns have, of course, produced further striking examples of good
design in their shopping-centres and groups of public buildings. Outside their
central areas the planning of the towns has necessarily been of a different order,
since different needs are being served, but it is interesting that, in most cases, the
construction of "neighbourhoods"—the principal sub-regions of the residential
part of the towns—has been on Garden City lines, with informal curving boundaries
and principal roads, and a scattered and irregular grouping of houses, wide grass
verges and carefully sited trees. The domestic buildings themselves are often a
modern version of the Georgian cottage, but without the symmetrical arrangement

Fig. 167.
Part of Town Square,
Stevenage

Fig. 168. A view in Town Square, Stevenage

Fig. 169. Model of Cumbernauld New Town

of doors and windows or the Classical detail. A fair criticism, now being made, of most New Towns is that the neighbourhoods are of such low density that they fall into the error, committed in Welwyn, of trying to be both towns and villages at once. This weakness is said to be overcome in Cumbernauld, one of the latest of the centres for rehousing large numbers of industrial workers—in this case an estimated 70,000, chiefly from the Glasgow area.

Cumbernauld is being sited on a broad hogsback of land about twelve miles to the north-east of the centre of Glasgow. The position seems to have been selected on the grounds that it will result in the minimum of interference with existing forms of land-use, or in other words because it is a place which, so far throughout history, has proved practically worthless to both man and beast. In winter—which is a long season in this part of Britain—this is a bleak place and provides a stiff test for town planners in their efforts to create an urban environment in what is something of a natural wilderness. The shape of the town is necessarily being governed to some extent by the site, and also by the decision to discard the town planning fashion of decentralisation into scattered neighbourhoods, in favour of a preference for a denser ratio of houses to land and a far greater dependence of all parts of the town on the principal shopping and business centre. This decision seems wise, both in view of the circumstances of the environment in which Cumbernauld is arising— a greater degree of crowding of the buildings being a way of ensuring shelter and of warding off the sense of exposure—and in the light of the experience of earlier New Towns and Garden Cities which, as has been shown, are now seen to be too diffuse, and to lack the cohesion that most older towns have achieved by gradual growth.

172

Against this general background the shaping of Cumbernauld New Town is being controlled by a decision of major importance with regard to internal communications. While most other urban areas, subject to a comprehensive plan of building in the post-war period, have stopped short, in their designing for the motor-car age, at one or more pedestrian precincts and foot-path communication between various parts of the neighbourhoods, in Cumbernauld it has been decided at the outset to work on the assumption that every family will ultimately possess a car and that these cars will be used even for very short distances of travel within the town. At the same time a network of foot-paths must be available for mothers with prams, children, and the old or infirm (and even, presumably, for any able-bodied who are so eccentric as still to like walking for its own sake). Given these various assumptions and starting-points, a town plan has emerged which is illustrated by the photograph of a model in the possession of Cumbernauld New Town Development Corporation (fig. 169).

The main difference between the ground-plan of Cumbernauld and that of a place like Welwyn (fig. 152) is that at Cumbernauld the houses are in quite tightly-packed groups with, usually, paved ways between them, whereas at Welwyn the wide grass verges, following the lines of the roads, separate the houses into long flowing streams. Trees and a few boulders and patches of heather are being kept in the Scottish New Town, but the main plan for open spaces is to group them in belts around the periphery of the main residential area. Everything is thus set for the modelling of a town in shapes which suggest neighbourliness and even a bit of friendly congestion, and time must be allowed before the scheme is judged in full. So far, there are signs that the scheme is beginning to achieve the social aim of a friendly community composed of people used to the close proximity of neighbours in the tenement-dwellings of Glasgow. What is not so clear is that the architectural achievement is as successful as the social one, and yet design is, in the long run, of paramount importance to the venture.

Cumbernauld seems to have set itself the aesthetic task of extending the possibilities of the current mode of building-design to embrace the problem of re-creating the feeling of a crowded hill-top town, fishing village or medieval city. This is a most exciting aim; it is also one well suited to realisation in a country of rugged natural forms and simple, firm shapes in the traditional domestic buildings. In some cases, in Cumbernauld, crouched buildings, in the design of which care has been taken to maintain privacy and at the same time to secure good views and the maximum of sunlight, make successful units. Unfortunately these have, too often, been repeated in straight, short terraces which lack the sweep and the distinction of fine long rows, and at the same time fail to provide the quaintness and inviting quality of a winding street in a hill-village (fig. 170). Elsewhere, there are considerable stretches of housing in designs of a spartan simplicity. Some of these seem to deny the need for any kind of aesthetic appeal (fig. 171), and although the Cumbernauld Development Corporation has claimed that, in these parts of the town, a particularly happy community sense has been created, the success of a piece of town-building cannot be judged in these terms alone, otherwise there would seem to be no good reason for replacing slums, which are traditionally the friendliest of places, with any kind of new environment.

Fig. 170. A group of new houses at Cumbernauld

At the time of writing, there are in existence extensive plans, on paper, for the rebuilding of parts of our older towns and cities. Only a few of these are anywhere near completion on the ground, but ten years from now, huge urban areas will have become unrecognisably altered. Our towns thus stand on the threshold of a revolution, and we can, at this point, take but a brief look at some of the pointers to the way in which things will go. The much-discussed rebuilding at Coventry is an example of almost total re-creation of the centre of a town on a cleared site, for where the bombs had left some remnants of the old city, the bulldozer completed the process. Coming early to the problem, the war-struck city got away to a flying start and boldly went for a plan of separating its people from its traffic. The design of the first of the new buildings is not of a very high standard. It is generally the case, in Britain, that architecture in the immediate post-war period was backward-looking, and it was not until about 1955 or so that a more convincing contemporary style was adopted. Coventry's early start was, therefore, a little unfortunate, and by comparison her neighbour Birmingham has emerged as a city which is taking the tide in her affairs at full flood.

174

Fig. 171. More housing, Cumbernauld

The rebuilding of the Bull Ring (the site of a traditional market) shows the progress that Birmingham has made in the field of contemporary town design. No concession has been made to preservationism here, and some may feel that there are Victorian buildings, of perhaps second-class order, that would have been worth keeping. But there is no denying the brilliance of the scheme of roads and buildings that is emerging. The most striking thing about this piece of town planning is that, although it contains major roads carrying heavy volumes of traffic, the skilful exploitation of the site and the variation of the levels of both pedestrian-ways and roads makes the interweaving of the two segregated lines of communication a stimulating achievement. To watch the flow of traffic from a broad pavement or a raised boulevard, and yet feel that you are not called upon to try to cross it, is like standing on Westminster Bridge enjoying the busy activity of the Thames. Complete abolition of a majority of vehicles from the crowded parts of towns is often necessary, but in cities of a million inhabitants it is neither possible nor desirable. In Birmingham it seems as if the design of the great new curving streets is intended to make modern road transport perform a dramatic role like the commerce of many a great river, canalised between fine buildings, in the historic cities of the world. This achievement should be well marked, for it is something quite different from the construction of two horizontal decks for two different worlds to live on.

175

Fig. 172. Buildings at The Bull Ring, Birmingham

The Bull Ring development is not only a triumph of engineering; it also has buildings which, both individually and in their grouping, are of outstanding merit. Fine, bold lines, uncompromising sweeps of façade, beautifully balanced verticals and horizontals—these are all in the best tradition of modern design, and they have a unity of composition and an originality of style that make them a highly sensitive work of urban art (fig. 172). Enveloping the old nineteenth-century core of Birmingham and, it is to be hoped, maintaining the best of it—for there is some noble building in and around Victoria Square (fig. 111, Chapter 7)—a very extensive scheme of modernisation is in the course of execution, of which the Bull Ring region is only a part. Likewise, in other big cities, developments are afoot, including the Barbican Scheme in the City of London, and the Central Area Plan for Liverpool, of a size and comprehensiveness that will make totally new townscapes come into being. In Sheffield, Leeds, Newcastle and Manchester, housing schemes, office and commercial buildings and university extensions are also transforming the scene, and almost no sizeable town lacks a tower block or two to mark the mid-twentieth century. The idea of planning towns as whole compositions is gaining ground, especially in the big industrial cities where the worst kind of nineteenth-century working-class housing invites a "clean-sweep" attitude, but there is a long way to go before a proper concern is shown for the problem of integrating new building with existing environments, particularly in the chief historic cities, and the multitude of fine small towns and large villages of this country.

In addition to its place in the building of New Towns and the reconstruction of parts of old ones, the contemporary phase of design is having its impact, though with less emphatic results, on the still-growing suburban landscape. Step by step and field by field, in spite of the Green Belts which have been drawn optimistically, and sometimes chokingly, around large conurbations, and in spite of the agricultural land which, admittedly, is not a greater priority than residential space, urban accretion continues steadily to add its concentric zones to our towns. This is being done with "planning consent", but, in the case of the products of private enterprise, hardly as a result of a creative planning policy. Thus the shapes of these parts of our towns are often rather fortuitous, though they are none the less interesting. A complicated process is under way whereby, at the edge of present settlements, former fields, pieces of common land, parts of landed estates and so on, are being laid out either as new council estates or as fairly self-contained units, with an access road or two, and rather closely-packed bungalows or semi-detached houses disposed according to the general convenience of a private builder.

Typical examples of townscapes of this kind, which are being produced by both local authority and private development, are to be found at Weston-super-Mare, on the borders of the Bristol Channel. This largely Edwardian-looking seaside resort, with its characteristic grey stone houses of Carboniferous Limestone—decorated with the yellow Cotswold stone—has spread along the south side of Worlebury Hill and out on to the plain in a belt parallel to the long shore of Weston Bay. In the inter-war years, continued building helped to extend the town towards outlying villages like Uphill and Bleadon to the south, and Worle and Kewstoke to the north-east. By the beginning of the post-war building boom an extensive urban area

Fig. 173.
The outskirts of
Weston-super-Mare

already existed, and development then proceeded across the plain towards the Mendips and also caused the filling-in of the gaps still remaining between the town and the neighbouring villages. Local authority planning, which includes provision for a light-industrial area, and has schools and shops as essential parts of its schemes, has been mainly on the south-east side of Weston, and here the most recent developments have been on the Oldmixon Estate which is being extended to the foot of Bleadon Hill. The designing of this area has favoured unfenced front gardens, winding roads and back lanes, and house styles which are neither wholly modern nor wholly traditional. The treatment of the façades of terraces as one area of colour and texture, and the development of window-areas into bold rectangles by the addition of panels which carry the vertical lines of the window-frames up to the eaves, and down to the ground, hint at the contemporary Classical look: but the fairly steeply-pitched roofs, the irregular grouping of clusters and terraces, the tentative landscaping by means of flowering trees and amorphous green plots, and the choice of brick and tile as the principal building materials, presents a picture which is distinctly Romantic. The way in which this area extends from the edge of earlier council estates to add a recent but not a basically new element to the spreading town of Weston is illustrated in fig. 173.

Around the periphery of Weston the private housing developments have, for the most part, been of more piecemeal character than have those of the town council. Some current building schemes by private enterprise have adopted the suggestions of the local planning authority for treating small areas (covering several fields) as one unit, and, ignoring the old field boundaries, have given rise to road patterns and house-groups along "Garden City" lines. But usually new building goes on by converting one field at a time into a little estate of houses of similar general design, the styles striking a careful balance between anything riskily modern on the one hand, and anything overtly rustic or otherwise old-fashioned on the other. Fig. 174 shows a group of houses, occupying what was probably, until the recent past, a field of rough pasture. This little estate on Worlebury Hill demonstrates current modes in designs by the small private developer. Pre-cast stone, picture windows, green roof-tiles, dormers and rough-cast sections of walls mingle to make that semi-Romantic adaptation of new fashions which seems to suit the conservative taste and short pocket of the typical English family.

178

The contemporary phase of the British townscape thus presents us with some new and exciting things, together with a good deal which falls far short of the dramatic. What we are witnessing to-day, whatever its quality, is a part of the continuous process of British town building. Reconstruction at the heart of settlements is not something new; nor is encroachment on agricultural fields for new houses and places of work. Over and over again, in medieval and early modern times, our towns have been face-lifted; over and over again crowded sites have burst their bonds and spread into the once-rural landscape beyond. Each time this has happened the British townscape has taken on a new shape, employing the fashion of the day for the purpose. But each new element in the form of our towns shows a characteristic restraint in the use of this fashion, a restraint which at its worst can produce a provincial "semi-desert", thirsty for the flavour of true urban existence, but at its best is a contribution of real value to the recurrent process of designing towns for a people of temperate habit.

Fig. 174. A private estate at Worlebury Hill, Weston-super-Mare

12. *A Summing-Up*

PHOTOGRAPHS, maps and historical accounts can take us so far, in our attempt to understand and appreciate townscape, but no farther. It is only from its pavements, or from the top of its church tower, that the unique qualities that distinguish every town in Britain can be apprehended. However fully we may have studied a place before we actually see it, there are always some totally unexpected elements in its make-up which, when we come upon them "in the flesh", overpower all the other ideas which have been gained from analysis. The unexpectedness may result from the gentle undulations in the site of a town where we had anticipated absolute flatness, or from a billiard-table smoothness where we had "seen", in our minds, a wide basin or some minor irregularities of the surface. The scenery of a town may seem to be dominated, on first acquaintance, by red-tiled roofs, or by the stern greyness of everything—caused by the predominance of a local building-stone; or it may be the wide streets which strike us first, or the trolley-bus wires, or the frequency of neat little flower-beds, or the pit gear, or the cooling-towers, or the view of the countryside glimpsed through many gaps in the buildings. The impressions that a town may make are numberless, since each person will receive his impression in a different way, and in trying to account for many examples of the townscapes of Britain by means of descriptions and pictures an attempt has been made to re-create atmospheres which have been experienced at first hand.

In attempting to separate the various components of an involved composition, we find that, in pointing to one aspect of townscape, attention has been directed away from others that might be equally important. The townscapes in this book are associated with various periods of time; but towns are made up of many townscapes and one of the limitations of the method chosen here is that it cannot provide a full consideration of the synthesised shape which a town presents as a whole: British townscapes have been seen as "historic components", but the British town has been only briefly glimpsed. Again, there has been a tendency to ignore some very important details of the townscape through using, in each illustration, an example which covers a fairly extensive area of an existing town. Yet one or two buildings alone, especially when taken in conjunction with some well-known feature of a town's scenery, like a clock-tower, a monument or an ancient city wall, can express, powerfully, the town's morphological character. The town scene includes moving objects, too, which may be an essential part of its character. For example, the red buses of London and Manchester, in combination with darkened statuary, stained Portland stone, and pale leaves of the trees that survive in city parks, make up a kind of "big-city" townscape which is familiar to everyone, but is of a kind to which it has been impossible to do any justice in this book. And the almost complete omission of the townscape that is made—or, more correctly, unmade—by the directives to traffic and the shop-signs, by hoardings and other public advertisements—has also to be excused here, since it would make a subject for a book in itself and is receiving much attention elsewhere.

Nevertheless, the main theme of this book has been to trace, over a wide geographical field, the varied characteristics of urban design which were briefly glimpsed in the study of Dawlish (in Chapter 2). We have seen that British towns are often made up of small areas which date from before the year 1800, and from large ones which were built after that date. The early forms of a town have a significance out of proportion to the space they occupy in the present urban structure, since their influence has extended to subsequent periods of development, and some later forms—and especially the plan of streets—may derive from an older town which has disappeared. Old townscapes, with many medieval features, are rarely made up of complete survivals from the Middle Ages, and are generally so altered—in particular by the addition of Georgian fronts to houses—that they make a mixed type of scenery of their own, which is very common throughout Britain, especially in the smaller country towns. The English Renaissance produced a Classical townscape which survives in notable examples of the art of town design: these are usually fairly modest in scale and very refined in their details and proportions, and are mellowed to-day by the maturity of ancient trees that have added a touch of the Romantic to the formalism of the scene. Industrialism gave rise to towns which came under the influence of the steady alteration in taste which occurred throughout the nineteenth century. At the opening of that century, tenements of Classical design were being built, but were soon replaced, in the period of greatest urban expansion, by the small brick cottages for separate families that preserved some illusion of privacy and individualism, and which gradually changed in appearance from a poor imitation of the Georgian town house of the well-to-do to a place with a few superficial concessions to the Romantic revival, though in the public buildings and parks of the period there was a compensating opulence of style. The whole-hearted Romanticism of the Garden City builders, and the uncompromising asceticism of the best architects of the early years of the modern movement, made only a very short-term appeal to the British, and the townscape of the twentieth century became a scene of varied shapes resulting from the current revisions of Classical and Romantic ideas. Throughout the story of British townscapes there can therefore be traced the strong imprint of successive architectural fashions, while there is always present a native tendency to avoid the sensational and the extreme, sometimes to the point of becoming insipid, but often with a result that is highly civilised. In other words, the mixture of styles and the modest scale that were found in the sample study of Dawlish are seen to be characteristic of the majority of British towns.

Thus far there may be little disagreement with the main conclusions of a book which does no more than rewrite a story that is already plainly told in the streets and buildings all around us. But it is difficult to leave, without further comment, a subject which has more than purely academic interest. The word townscape involves, in addition to the sense in which it has been used here, the idea of human environment, and it surely matters profoundly that any judgments we make on the quality of our urban "home" shall be both informed and very carefully considered. We cannot afford to live to regret, at leisure, mistakes made in haste, in the name of such slogans as "urban renewal to meet the demands of the car-age". There are towns in Britain to-day where a landscape of industrial squalor surrounds a bright little shopping "centre", the building of which has achieved little more than the destruction of some rather pleasant old Georgian streets, and the repetition, only with much less artistry, of the actions of our forefathers when they put all the effort that might have been given to improving living conditions into raising a few show-pieces in the name of civic pride. Yet this passes as "Town Planning": can we not do better?

As a result of the foregoing study of the various kinds of town scenery that we inherit, it may be possible to make some comments, of a speculative kind, which will help us to pass judgments on the value of the existing townscape. To begin with, there can be little doubt that some good, and some bad, designing has occurred in towns at most times in their history—in fact in all periods from which sufficient evidence remains for us to pass any useful comment. The eighteenth century, for instance, has left behind a great extent of bare, undesigned and often quite hideous back-quarters of its domestic buildings as well as much beauty "out front". The mid-nineteenth century was responsible for some of our finest civic building—on which many towns are now glad to base part of their reputation—but it also bequeathed us the webs of heartless streets to which time and industrial dirt have added decay and gloom. The late nineteenth century and the Edwardian era repeated, with perhaps a little gloss, many of the follies which date from Victoria's reign—particularly in the field of poor domestic building—but this age was also one of the most creative periods in the history of townscape; it gave birth to the idea that cities could exist in a garden-like setting, and also to the seemingly very different view that buildings in towns should reflect the shapes and materials of a new industrial age. (Fig. 175 shows that these two ideas can, in fact, be reconciled quite pleasantly.) Thus we find that it would be most irresponsible to dismiss any one broad period of town-building as of no aesthetic value.

And so a survey of the kind that has been undertaken here forces one to speculate, to some small degree at least, on the question "What is good taste?"—as it applies to the design of towns. That ideas of good taste vary from period to period is obvious if we study any art; and this fact alone should make us very cautious indeed in making sweeping judgments about an age. It might, however, be allowed that, within a period in which one general kind of taste is favoured, there will be greater and lesser exponents of that taste. One useful way in which we can study urban design is to look for what we think is good of its kind, or for its period, rather than for something that, according to our own preconceived tenets, has some universal value. We shall then find, for example, that there are urban relics of the industrial

Fig. 175. A new factory building in Letchworth

Fig. 176. A side street in Salford, Manchester

age that have matured into something with a quality approaching the charm of a quiet country town (fig. 176) and that the unloved suburbs of our modern cities have surprises in store which, in their own way, are little "collectors' pieces" (fig. 177).

A further point which the analysis of townscapes—as survivals of past phases of taste—makes clear (and from which some useful conclusion may be drawn) is that, in each age, there have been supremely confident sponsors of a new and controversial style. Therefore, although there is so much good left to us from the past that we

Fig. 177. Linden Drive, suburban Leicester

ould be wrong to sweep all old things away just because they are old, it is equally ue that a lack of conviction about what is appropriate to the second half of the ventieth century will leave us with "the worst of both worlds". At the risk of re- eating what has already been said on this score, it must be stressed that, in Britain -day, while a good deal of New Town architecture shows bold and progressive vention, the rebuilding of parts of our older towns has mostly carried our love of ompromise to a point where it is no longer possible to recognise a style at all.

13*

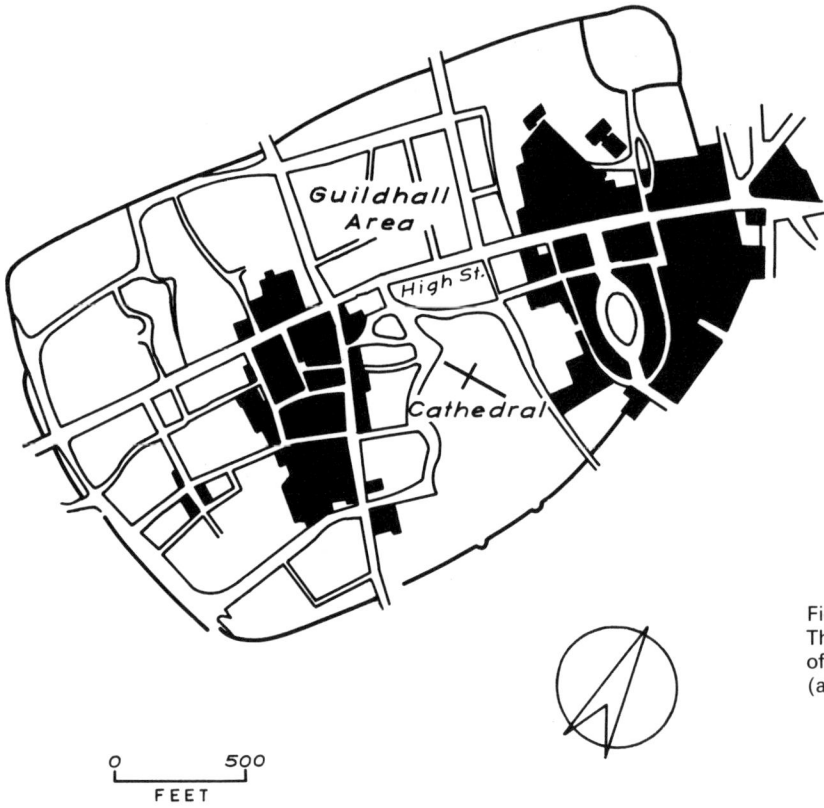

Fig. 178.
The blitzed areas
of central Exeter
(after Thomas Sharp)

Guildhall
Area

High St.

Cathedral

0   500
FEET

Fig. 179. The " Guildhall area " of Exeter, looking south

This state of affairs exists to-day in Exeter, a city which contains, still, a splendid record of building through the ages, but which has virtually no modern buildings of value in the centre of the town and is on the brink of decisions which may destroy many of those good things which date from the past. After the war, along with many towns and cities, Exeter started on the painful road of recovery following the bombing raids. In Exeter's case, one night of destruction—in 1942—razed two extensive areas of the centre of the city (fig. 178), and reduced to rubble some of the town's finest records of urban style—chiefly of the late medieval and Georgian periods. An excellent plan, by Dr. Thomas Sharp (published under the title "*Exeter Phoenix*"[1]), was prepared, at the invitation of the City Council, and some of this has now been carried out. Now of course no plan produced during the war years (and there were many of these plans, not only in the war-stricken cities but in industrial towns and in historic county capitals and elsewhere) could expect to foresee all that has subsequently happened; and Thomas Sharp's plan was no exception to this rule. But with regard to the principal practical problem in city centres, namely that of traffic congestion, the solutions offered in "*Exeter Phoenix*" were more far-reaching than the part of the plan so far completed in the city would suggest. So there is still reason to hope that the whole of the original road plan will be retained. If this is done, the way will be open for better things than have so far been accomplished in new buildings. Except by way of hints and proddings, a development plan cannot ensure that the kind of new buildings which will eventually be designed in a town are of a high order, and, in Exeter's case, the chance which the city had to make a fine modern city in the spaces cleared by the bombs has been lost, for these spaces are now filled with streets and buildings which make no advance on the quality achieved in London's Finchley Road.

Sad as this is, real tragedy lies ahead if the next phase of development is to take the form of any of the detailed plans which have so far been considered for replanning that part of central Exeter known as the Guildhall Area. This is a piece of the city, to the north of the Cathedral Close, which was left mostly intact by the bombing, and where there are survivals of buildings, and parts of buildings, from almost all the principal periods of construction in the city since Roman times. If there is a place where our studies of the jigsaw puzzle of town design can have practical value it is here, where the whole or a part of a street; a group of buildings on a corner; some interesting survivals in a back alley, and an occasional building of outstanding importance from an architectural or historical point of view, make up a final unique composition that looks protective, intimate and English and asks to be preserved. And there is plenty of room for new building: the nearby bus-station has been closed and leaves a large space vacant, and there are a number of structures in the area that are of such poor quality, architecturally, that their demolition would be an improvement in itself and would make room for new things (fig. 179). So in an area like this a study should be made of the individual buildings and then of groups of these buildings seen as compositions, thus bringing our knowledge of British townscapes in general to apply to a particular problem of modern town planning. This has been done in a preliminary survey, the results of which can be seen in fig. 180.

Fig. 180.
A pilot survey
of building quality
in the Guildhall
area of Exeter

Legend:

- (A) Outstanding
- (B) Very Good
- (C) Good
- (D) Poor
- Sheds, Outhouses etc.
- Demolished

0   200
FEET

R.F.

Map labels: Northernhay Street, City Wall, Bus Station, Paul Street, St. Pancras Church, North Street, Goldsmith Street, Queen Street, Waterbeer Street, Guildhall High Street

70' 80' 90' 100' 110' 120' 130' 140'

The Guildhall Area of Exeter has little bits of townscape of almost every period —old irregular Romantic houses which are medieval in plan and in a large part of their structure; the Guildhall itself, of early Renaissance style; Georgian house-fronts and windows; Victorian blocks of shops in stucco; a fine Grecian-style public building; a good red-brick corner-piece dating from about the beginning of the nt century, and—in the middle of it all—a small parish church of dignified city. Some examples of this fascinating collection of fragments—which have achieved a very real unity with the passage of time—are shown in figs. 181, 182 and 183. A number of plans put forward by property companies, for dealing with the Guildhall Area, have been submitted to the City Council but, at the time of writing, none has been approved. Not one of these plans has considered rehabilitating a large part of the region though one or two, in what seems to be a concession to local trading interests, have suggested retaining some of the larger shops for the time being. What is noticeable is that all the plans make provision for retaining the Guildhall and St. Pancras Church, and some would keep the Civic Hall, but all these buildings would then be stranded in an environment totally alien to them—"embalmed" for the sake of some semi-dormant social conscience which feels that to have one or two well-preserved bodies around the place is good for the soul. The reason for keeping a few monuments is, of course, in practical terms, simply that they are what is called "listed"—that is, that they appear in Grades I or II on the Ministry of Housing and Local Government's list of "Buildings of Architectural or Historic Interest". If ever there was a good idea that went wrong it was this attempt to catalogue showpieces while leaving out the groups of buildings which make good townscape; for the Ministry's lists, throughout the country, as well as at Exeter, encourage the very thing which they are presumably designed to prevent—that is the idea that it is unnecessary to think before pulling something down; for whatever does not appear on the lists can be dismissed forthwith as worthless, by a development authority, while that same authority salves its conscience and wards off all charges of philistinism by pointing proudly to a few "museum pieces", labelled "do not touch".

Fig. 181. Part of the High Street with the Guildhall, Exeter

Fig. 182. A scene in Goldsmith Street, Exeter

Fig. 183. (*opp.*) Part of Waterbeer Street, Exeter

The study of townscapes elsewhere in Britain shows clearly that Exeter's Guild-hall Area has both a fine inheritance and immense possibilities for the present age. There is not the slightest need here for conflict between the preservationist and the progressive, for a large part of this region could be kept, while leaving plenty of room for new buildings. What is more, the challenging task of trying to fit buildings to the scale of the old ones, without copying their style, could result meaningful use of the potentialities of modern methods of construction. The

tects of the new Exeter have a chance to employ some of the shapes which are tentatively being explored nowadays—shapes which hint at a new style of Baroque, or
even at another "twist" in Gothic Revivalism (figs. 184 and 185)—in a form which
will accord with the harmonious mixture of styles which is found in this very British
town.

Fig. 184. A "Modern Gothic" form of building: St. Vincent's Chapel,
         Coyoacán, Mexico

Fig. 185. The Shopping Centre, Windward City, Kaneohe, Hawaii

This brief example of a city in which the survey of townscape, as well as the listing of individual buildings, should play a part in contemporary planning, leads us back to the aim that has been pursued in these pages. The chief concern of this study of townscapes has been to show that areas of a town with common characteristics of design have a very real existence and that they play a major part in the general form of the town. Just as small social groups exist within larger communities, so our type of townscape exists as part of something larger. The atmosphere to be found in a part of a town where there are several streets of similar form, in which houses of one period of design stand together, creates an environment of a very important kind especially for those for whom it has always been home. The immediate urban surroundings have a profound effect on most of us especially in the impressionable years of childhood. Like many things that had a stronger meaning for us in the days when some of our senses were much sharper than they are now, the shapes, colours and textures of the part of the town where we lived made up a world which was experienced with intense emotion. The boundaries of the little worlds of the kind that have been called townscapes in this book are defined in a rather more sophisticated way than were the limits which we instinctively set to the piece of the home-town that was "ours": but the qualities of a townscape have to be sought out by means of the same kind of intimate contact as we experienced in the streets where we grew up. Only on foot—not always a comfortable form of progression in modern towns—and only through the eyes, can townscapes be first properly located and then fully explored. Moreover, this search must be made not only in the tourist haunts and the great cities, but also in towns with an atmosphere created by a hundred and fifty years of industrial sweat, or in the cul-de-sacs of suburbia where no traveller has paused before to take a second look. Above all it is only with a sense of sympathy for these places as works of "man the artist" as well as of "man the builder" that we should presume to judge them.

193

Notes

C<small>HAPTER</small> 1: Introduction

1. Moral judgments are included here as well as aesthetic ones (if indeed these two things can be separated) because what we feel to be artistically right is usually bound up with what we feel to be proper in the moral sense. The extent to which the female body should be covered is obviously in part a moral question, and so, in a sense, is the extent to which a building should be imposing or restrained, exposed or hidden, soaring to heaven or clinging to earth. Whether or not we agree with the details of Lewis Mumford's thesis in *The City in History* (London, 1961), there can be little doubt that his main proposition in that book—that the shape of cities derives in some part from the moral outlook of the societies which produce them—is correct.
2. It may seem to some readers that, in this book, the word architecture is applied to buildings of very low quality. But there seems no better word to use when discussing the aesthetic qualities of a building even if our private opinion of those qualities is not a high one.
3. The word "design" is always used here in that sense referred to in the *Concise Oxford Dictionary* as "the artistic groundwork", and not in its more general sense as a "mental plan".
4. A. E. Smailes, *Some Reflections on the Geographical Description and Analysis of Townscapes*, Transactions of the Institute of British Geographers, London, 1955, p. 99.
5. Ibid., p. 100.
6. Gordon Cullen, *Townscape*, London, 1961, p. 9.
7. It has been decided to exclude industrial "landscapes" from the study, on grounds of convenience, but they are obviously essential parts of many towns and would make a fascinating subject for a separate book.
8. An attempt has been made to cover a fair sample of geographical regions in Britain with these examples. Unfortunately the scope of the subject is such that ideal coverage is impossible to realise, as readers will soon be aware, but it is to be hoped that they will be generous in their criticisms of the deficiencies.

C<small>HAPTER</small> 2: The National Townscape

1. The subject "The Englishness of English Art" was chosen by Nikolaus Pevsner for a series of lectures broadcast by the B.B.C. in 1955, published in *The Listener*, and later as a single volume with the same title, London, 1956.
2. Pierre George, *Précis de géographie urbaine*, Paris, 1961, p. 33.
3. Lewis Mumford, *The City in History*, London, 1961, Chs. 12 and 13, and *The Culture of Cities*, London, 1938, Ch. 2.

194

4. The *Oxford Dictionary* is useful when applying the term Romantic to townscapes. Its definition is "preferring grandeur or picturesqueness or passion or irregular beauty to finish and proportion, subordinating whole to parts, or form to matter".

5. The terms "Regency" and "Queen Anne" are often employed to describe the style of architecture which was roughly contemporary with the later years of the reign of George III and the reign of Queen Anne. They are not entirely satisfactory terms and will not be used here as accepted terminology.

6. No satisfactory general term exists to define the overall style of contemporary architecture. The style is Classical in the sense that it is concerned with precise formal relationships, but it lacks the emphasis on symmetry that has been a major feature of earlier Classical movements, and makes positive use of strong contrasts of the scale of masses, and the direction of line. It is these characteristics that are summed up in the word "cubist" as used here.

7. Cob is the name used in Devon for the local version of mud-walling. The materials used to make walls of cob include earth, dung, straw and grit; these are mixed with water to form a concrete which was trodden in a prepared mould and allowed to set.

Chapter 3: The Region and the Town

1. For example, David Ward, in *The Pre-Urban Cadaster and the Urban Pattern of Leeds* (Annals of the Association of American Geographers, June 1962), has shown that the shape of groups of "back-to-back" houses in Leeds has been determined, in part, by the pattern of field-boundaries which existed before the streets were laid out.

2. E. M. Jope, in *Studies in Building History*, London, 1961, p. 197, considers that difficulties of medieval transport have been over-emphasised—but he is referring to the building of large houses, churches, etc.

3. John Summerson, *Georgian London*, Pelican edn., London, 1962, p. 79.

4. The very hard sandstone, of the Carboniferous series, found in this area.

5. W. Douglas Simpson, "The Tower-Houses of Scotland", Ch. 12 of *Studies in Building History*, E. M. Jope, London, 1961.

6. A. K. Wickham, *The Villages of England*, London, 1932, p. 25.

Chapter 4: Late-Medieval Town Scenes

1. E.g. the house of Horace Walpole, at Twickenham, known as Strawberry Hill, which gave its name to a style of Gothic building.

2. Even the most far-reaching of the current road proposals for Exeter do not greatly change the ancient pattern of streets.

3. W. G. Hoskins, *Two Thousand Years in Exeter*, p. 20.

4. M. R. G. Conzen, *Alnwick, Northumberland, A Study in Town Plan Analysis*, Transactions of the Institute of British Geographers, Vol. 27, London, 1960.

5. Ibid., p. 16.

6. Ibid., p. 47.

7. A. K. Wickham, *The Villages of England*, London, 1932, p. 25.

8. F. Lingard Ranson, *Lavenham, Suffolk*, 1958, p. 42.

9. Ibid., p. 44.

10. Ibid., p. 48.

11. *The Black Book of Warwick*, transcribed and edited by Thomas Kemp, 1898.

12. Ibid., p. x.

13. Ibid., p. xiv.

CHAPTER 5: The Renaissance in British Townscape

1. R. Carrier and O. L. Dick, *The Vanished City*, London, 1957.
2. The Vitruvian writers (who lived mainly in the sixteenth century) were a group of advocates of the principles of Vitruvius—whose treatise on Classical building survives from antiquity. Vitruvius, and his successors in the Renaissance, advocated town-plans of the utmost rigidity and symmetry as in the plan of Palma Nova, not far from Venice (see fig. 52).
3. Walter Ison, *The Georgian Buildings of Bath*, London, 1948, p. 46.
4. John Summerson, *Georgian London*, London, 1962, Ch. 1.
5. See I. G. Lindsay, *Georgian Edinburgh*, Edinburgh, 1948, pp. 12, 13.

CHAPTER 6: The Renaissance in British Townscape (*continued*)

1. The population of Lavenham was 1,489 in 1961.
2. See J. M. Howell, The birth and growth of Aberayron, *Trans. Card. Antiq. Soc.*, Vol. 4, 1926.
3. E. W. Gilbert, *Brighton, Old Ocean's Bauble*, London, 1954, p. 91.
4. Edward Mitchell, Map of Cheltenham, 1806, Cheltenham Reference Library.
5. John Goding, *Norman's History of Cheltenham*, p. 269.
6. Alfred Adlard, Map of Cheltenham, 1853, Cheltenham Reference Library.
7. See Brian Little, *Cheltenham*, London, 1951, p. 31.
8. Goding, op. cit., p. 561.
9. John Summerson, *Georgian London*, London, 1962, Ch. 13.
10. Colin Buchanan, *Journ. T.P. Inst.*, Feb. 1964, p. 53.
11. Summerson, op. cit., p. 22.

CHAPTER 7: New Towns of the Industrial Age

1. The best survey of nineteenth-century town development, seen as both a social and a geographical process, is probably William Ashworth's *The Genesis of Modern British Town Planning*, London, 1954.
2. Leland, in 1538, described Manchester as "the best builded . . . and most populous town of all Lancashire". *Leland's Itinerary*, 3rd ed., 1768.
3. D. H. Lawrence, *Sons and Lovers*, London, 1913.
4. This figure includes Great and Little Bolton.
5. C. H. Saxelby (ed.), *Bolton Survey*, Bolton, 1953, p. 90.
6. Ordnance Survey 1/528 (44 feet to 1 inch). Copy in the Town Planning Department, the Town Hall, Merthyr.
7. The site of Cyfarthfa Works (marked "pram and toy factory") can be seen on the map (fig. 96).
8. These are seen to the south of Georgetown (fig. 96).
9. Similar phases to those which, in terms of chapel architecture are called "Early Classic" and "Classic", by Anthony Jones, *Chapel Architecture in Merthyr Tydfil*, 1962, p. 10.
10. Later examples of the well-known work of George Cadbury, Joseph Rowntree and W. H. Lever will have similar importance.
11. See *New Lanark: Historical Background*, a document published by the New Lanark Association Ltd., Edinburgh, 21 Nov. 1963.
12. W. Davidson, *A History of Lanark and Guide to the Scenery*, 1828, p. 160.
13. Designed for her, by Thomas Cubitt, on the Isle of Wight.
14. Ashworth, op. cit., p. 38.

CHAPTER 8: Transitional Town Styles

1. Bannister Fletcher, *A History of Architecture on the Comparative Method*, London, 1943, p. 858.
2. Percy Russell, *A History of Torquay*, Torquay, 1960, p. 160.
3. Lady Bell, *At the Works, a Study of a Manufacturing Town*, 1907. See Asa Briggs, *Victorian Cities*, London, 1964, p. 273.

CHAPTER 9: Romantic Town Scenery

1. John Gloag, *Victorian Taste*, London, 1962, p. 98.
2. Osbert Sitwell, *Low Tide*, in *Alive—Alive Oh! and other stories*, London, 1947, p. 148.
3. Sir Reginald Blomfield, R.A., *Richard Norman Shaw*, London, 1940, p. 33.
4. These two styles persisted with remarkable vigour throughout the twentieth century in housing schemes.
5. Lewis Mumford, intro. essay in *Garden Cities of Tomorrow*, by Ebenezer Howard, London, 1960, p. 32.
6. C. B. Purdom, *The Building of Satellite Towns*, London, 1949, p. 62.

CHAPTER 10: Romantic Town Scenery (*continued*)

1. F. J. Osborn, Preface to *Garden Cities of Tomorrow*, by Ebenezer Howard, London, 1960, p. 14. (Note: between 1898 and 1944 Great Britain's population increased by 11 millions, and the number of dwellings by 4–5 millions.)
2. W. Ashworth, *Genesis of Modern British Town Planning*, London, 1954, p. 163.
3. Co-partnership societies became a popular way of ensuring a good standard in reasonably-priced housing in the early years of this century. Ashworth explains their methods as follows: "The co-partnership method was to raise capital from both investors and prospective tenants and to limit interest to 4 per cent or 5 per cent. The tenant members' share of the profits was credited to them in shares, not in cash, and any capital was paid to the tenants as a dividend on rental . . . ." (Ashworth, op. cit., pp. 158, 159). Societies of this type, through the Garden City Development Company at Hampstead, employed twenty (or so) architects who agreed to harmonise their individual or group-buildings, into the general plan.
4. Hampstead Tenants Ltd., *Cottages with Gardens for Londoners*, pp. 6–7 (quoted in Ashworth, op. cit., p. 161).
5. Henrietta Barnett, *The Story of the Growth of the Hampstead Garden Suburb, 1907 to 1928*, 1928, p. 7.
6. W. G. Hoskins, *Leicestershire*, London, 1957, p. 72.
7. Robert Guy Waddington, *Leicester, the Making of a Modern City*, Leicester, 1931, p. 85.
8. Ibid., p. 87.

CHAPTER 11: The Modern Town

1. The Bauhaus was an art school in Weimar, created by Walter Gropius and opened in 1919. "It was at the same time a laboratory for handicraft and for standardisation; a school and a workshop. It comprised, in an admirable community spirit, architects,

master craftsmen, abstract painters, all working for a new spirit in building." Nikolaus Pevsner, *Pioneers of Modern Design*, London, 1960, p. 38.

2. Frederick Gore, *Abstract Art*, London, 1956, plate 5.
3. Ibid., notes for plate 5.
4. Stevenage Development Corporation, *Stevenage New Town* (pamphlet).

CHAPTER 12: A Summing-Up

1. Thomas Sharp. *Exeter Phoenix*, London, 1946.